Puppy Development Guide

PUPPY 101 for Dog Lovers

The Secrets to Puppy Training without Force, Fear, and Fuss

Tim Carter

Founder MyGermanShepherd.Org

Edition 10

ISBN: 1482760673

ISBN-13: 978-1482760675

Disclaimer

Every dog is special, through its unique genetical heritage, living environment, and personal treatment by its owner or handler, as well as prior and current human and animal contacts.

Accordingly, no suggestions given to a dog owner or handler can ever be right for every dog and its owner regardless of the individual circumstances. It is your and your dog's individual circumstances that may or may not make a certain form of training, care, or remedy successful in your case.

You are encouraged to consciously observe your puppy and adult dog in order to recognize any adverse development as soon as possible, and to apply your own common sense to complement the suggestions made in this book, in light of your individual situation.

Neither the publisher nor the author can be held accountable, neither for the favorable implications of applying any suggestion made in this book, nor for the unfavorable implications. It is your dog's individual situation that will determine the success of any and every suggestion made in this book, and your dog's individual situation as well as your opinion will change with time.

DEDICATION

This book is dedicated to all young and old dogs
that end up in a shelter, every day

We all can make a difference

I do with this book
And you do by recommending it

In the name of those dogs I've seen suffering in
shelters and high kill kennels: Thanks!

Contents

How to Use this Book 15

Why You Need This Book 20

Getting a Puppy 29

Where to Get a Puppy 34

Backyard Breeders *35*

Pet Stores *37*

Puppy Mill Breeders *38*

Purebred Breeders *39*

Dog Shelters and Breed Rescue Centers *41*

What Do I Need for a New Puppy? 44

How to Puppy-Proof Your House *45*

Prepare a Place to Rest and Sleep *47*

Prepare a Place to Eat and Drink *51*

Puppy Safekeeping *54*

Puppy Grooming *57*

Get a Variety of Quality Toys *59*

Requirements of Quality Puppy Toys 60

Variety of Puppy Toys 61

The Right Mindset *64*

Bringing Home a New Puppy 67

Puppy Development Timeline 68

Litter Socialization *69*

Family Socialization *70*

Puberty *72*

Adolescence *74*

Puppy Vaccination 76

When to Start Puppy Training 83

Right Age to Start Puppy Training *83*

Right Time for Puppy Training *85*

Solving All the Common Puppy and Dog Behavior Problems! 90

The PRIME SECRET about Dogs 92

How to Become the *Accepted* Pack Leader 100

Puppy Attention Seeking *102*

How to Ignore the *Right* Way 104

Puppy Feeding Routine *108*

What to Do if Our Pup is Not Calm During Gesture Eating? 110

What if Our Pup Later is on 3 Meals a Day?. 111

And What if Our Pup is Not Calm During Several Consecutive Meal Times? 112

Combining the Feeding Routine with Bite Inhibition Training 115

Puppy Leash Training *117*

Puppy Collars 118

SSCD 120

Short Leash Training 122

Long Leash Training 125

The Recall 131

Reward Types 136

The NO-Force, NO-Fear, NO-Fuss Puppy Training 139

The ONLY 'Punishment' You'll Ever Need ... 142

Collar Freeze *146*

Isolation *149*

How to Best Socialize a Puppy 154

How to Train Our Puppy to Remain Calm *158*

How to Train Our Puppy to Intervene *162*

Bite Inhibition Training *166*

The Importance of Puppy Play and Play-Fighting *169*

Training Consistency 171

Puppy Development Little Helpers 173

Commands Little Helper *174*

Feeding Routine Little Helper *176*

Leash Training Little Helper *177*

Socialization Little Helper *178*

Behavior Modification Little Helper *182*

House Training a Puppy 184

Puppy Food *187*

Puppy Meal Times *193*

Puppy Feeding Routine *195*

8 Secrets to Housebreaking a Puppy in 7 Days or Less *196*

Puppy Crate Training *202*

10 Most Common Mistakes When Crate Training 203

10 Success Steps to Train a Puppy to Use its Crate Voluntarily 206

Puppy Leash Training *214*

Puppy Behavior Training *215*

Puppy Behavior Training 216

Puppy Chewing *218*

Puppy Scratching *222*

Puppy Digging *223*

How We Train Our Dog to Respect a Barrier 225

Puppy Barking *230*

Barking for Attention 231

Anxiety Barking 232

Alarm Barking 235

Puppy Whining *237*

Puppy Jumping *243*

Puppy Mouthing and Nipping *247*

Mouthing 248

Nipping 249

Why Controlled Mouthing and Nipping is Great 250

How to Stop Uninvited Mouthing and Nipping 251

How to Avoid to Stop Mouthing and Nipping Altogether 253

Puppy Biting *255*

How to Stop a Puppy from Biting 256

How to Stop Puppy Biting Immediately 257

Why is Isolation so Effective? 258

How to Stop Puppy Biting Proactively 260

Puppy Aggression *261*

Forms of Aggression 261

Eliminating Aggression 263

Puppy Training -v- Relationship Building 265

Puppy 101 in a Nutshell 268

More Books by the Same Author 271

Not to Forget! 277

How to Use this Book

I will not hold you up with a long introduction, because the initial plan was to make this a 10-pages-short(!) summary of our NO-Force, NO-Fear, NO-Fuss Puppy Training - or as we call it internally 'Puppy Training without 3F'. It was meant for our members at mygermanshepherd.org to help them with their dog, young or old (membership is free).

But then it turned out as a 120-pages *book*, apparently I couldn't hold myself back! - That was Edition 1 back in February 2013. Meanwhile we are at Edition 10 with more than twice as much content! Anyway, if it helps you it will make your dog happy too.

One major note though regarding **links** in this book: Throughout the entire book the focus is on helping you through relevant links, like we do on our breed rescue site mygermanshepherd.org - the largest breed authority site in the world.

Book-internal links

The abundance of cross-links should allow you to use this **Puppy 101** as **reference guide**, moving around as you like.

Book-external links

Many of these links lead to additional content for you. Primarily to our (normally members-only) *Periodicals*, most of which are extensively researched and comprehensive discussions of a specific topic.

Indeed, *so much* extra content, that - had I incorporated the linked content into this book - it would now have 1640 pages(!) - which would probably put off many potential readers. That's why I decided to link the extra content instead, such that whenever you want, you can visit the linked webpages at your own choice to deepen your understanding.

Obviously, the linked Periodicals are helpful to you regardless which breed of dog or mix you have - *unless* we specifically state in one of those Periodicals that a certain point relates to the German Shepherd dog only. So, *do* make use of all the additional linked content, because they give you incredible more value above and beyond the limited space in this book! Okay?

All other external links are to remedies or articles on other websites. In case of remedy links, most of the time these point to Amazon, namely whenever Amazon offers the item *and* is the cheapest source (which is generally the case since they have the biggest buying power globally, and many vendors use Amazon as sales platform for their own items).

Note that the majority of dog products are being developed and marketed where the majority of pet dogs live: 78 million in the USA! Hence our default remedy links point to amazon.com (and I have done the same in this book). But what if you live in Canada, or you want to gift the item to your sister in the UK who has a dog too?

Then you would need to get the eBook, which uses cute flags to help you find the right item in any Amazon locale (so many links wouldn't be possible in a print book). Thus, instead of say:

Nutramax Dasuquin with MSM (mygermanshepherd .org/go/nutramax-msm) - which is without doubt the *top* remedy for dog mobility problems(!) -

...the eBook would show: Nutramax Dasuquin with MSM (like we do it on our website). The links embedded in each cute flag give eBook readers the freedom to choose their preferred supplier (I love freedom). Nice side effect: The flags also lighten up the text and they document that our world is increasingly interconnected - certainly for dogs.

Oh, and one minor note regarding the high number of editions: In the past, whenever I noticed that, with hindsight, I should have written something else or something better, I felt I should. Thus, I issued a new edition.

HOWEVER: Not least our site members convinced me that I must stop optimizing my books, and I should rather focus on new things. At long last I agreed and vowed to myself to do just that (it really is terribly hard for perfectionists to 'let go' - it *is* an illness). So now, this edition 10 shall be the last (I hope). *Unless* I find something so bad that I feel I *have* to issue another edition... - Let's see.

Special Note for the Print Edition

Obviously with a print book the biggest disadvantage is that you cannot simply click on a linked word or image to jump to another book location, or to see the linked remedies, articles, or our site's Periodicals.

To give you access to the book-internal cross-references and linked extras nonetheless, I have painstakingly added page numbers and web addresses (URLs) to the relevant text locations. Took me ages, but I expect it will help you enormously when you seek more detail in future. Just note that due to the print process the page references can get slightly off track.

All URLs have hard line breaks, so that you can type them exactly as you see them (just without the line break). Example: mygermanshepherd.org/go/stypti
c-powder

Please accept that all other hyphenation in this book is done automatically by Microsoft Word.

Why You Need This Book

You see there are *hundreds* of dog and puppy training and care books on the market. And you probably own a few already if you've had dogs before.

However, I myself have read way more than a hundred dog *training* books alone, so I am confident to say: All books you find on dog training are based on **Obedience Training** - as if it was the holy grail to owning a dog. It is *not.* It is *because* so many dogs are only obedience-trained that we have so many dogs ending up in shelters!

Obedience Training really is no more than the *baseline* of dog ownership:

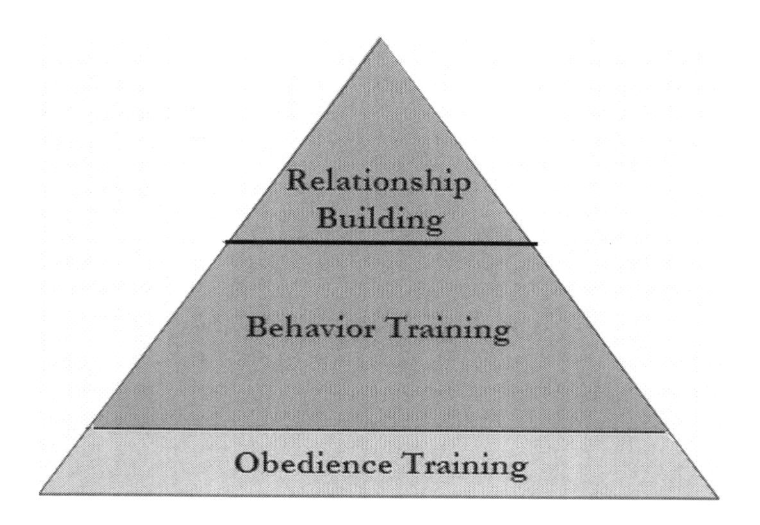

To build the best relationship with your dog, the major part of all dog training *needs* to be **Behavior Training**. So let's briefly look at what I mean.

The whole idea of **Obedience Training** is based on a Master-Servant mindset (1). The dog owner or trainer (Master) gives a command (2), and the dog or puppy (the servant) has to obey (3):

What's often covered up (in the above image too), is the necessary element of enforcement (4). These four constituents describe **Obedience Training**.

The enforcement in Obedience Training is one of the 3 F's: Force, Fear, Foods. Typically it's a combination.

- Force: eg tearing and dragging a leashed dog down the road, employing a choke collar or electronic collar, hitting or kicking the dog, shaking the dog by the collar, or being the repetitive type of person: "Sit" - "SIT" - "SIT!" - "I said SIIIT!!" - "SIT DOWN NOW for God's sake!!!"
- Fear: eg intimidating the dog with yelling, giving our face the really angry look, or raising the arm for that unmistakable threat of imminent action (with or without something in hand)
- Foods: eg *luring* the dog by waving a tasty morsel, or *bribing* the dog with food treats into doing what we want

More of this 'helicopter view' on Obedience Training you can find here: mygermanshepherd.org/periodical/obedience-training-pros-and-cons

---

Instead of focusing on Obedience Training with its 3 F's (Force, Fear, Foods) to enforce the commands such that the dog obeys, at mygermanshepherd.org we are beyond that. We focus on Behavior Training.

The whole idea of **Behavior Training** is that dogs are best trained through our own behavior. Ie we behave (1) in a way that motivates the dog (2) to behave the way we want, because adult dogs (3) closely observe our body language anyway (4). These four constituents describe **Behavior Training**.

Note that **adult dogs** intensely focus on our behavior - much more than on any commands we could give!

Puppies still focus on play, they don't yet interprete our behavior so much, our body language. Hence, puppies need more clear directions (commands) than adult dogs do. Still, any commands should be in addition to unambiguous behavior from us.

This is where practically all dog books on the market fail: They are still on level 1 of dog training: **Obedience Training**. The reader of the book and the client of the dog trainer learns how to use and how to enforce *commands*, but the dog owner's behavior speaks a different language: Now the puppy and adult dog alike are *confused* by the ambiguous potpourri of commands and body language!

This results in the familiar situations:

- The dog (and a puppy all the more) almost freezes (stands still and switches between looking around and looking at the owner), and visibly struggles to understand what the dog owner *really* wants

- One time the dog follows the owner's command exactly, but another time the dog doesn't, and the owner is perplexed about the dog's inconsistency

- The owner has to repeat the command multiple times, still the dog or puppy doesn't do as told, instead the dog just continues its action (or stays where it is), as if the owner had not said anything.

Sounds familiar? Of course it does. These are the *typical* situations all dog owners (and even dog trainers) are facing - every day!

And the reason for the dog's non-compliance always is one of these:

1. The dog or puppy is confused what the owner wants!

2. The dog believes that (s)he is the Pack leader who decides what needs to be done right now!

Or shorter, in "dog language" so to say:

1. "What do you want?"
2. "I tell you what I want!"

For *both* reasons it is crucial that our own behavior is unambigious. Already with a puppy. It is crucial that our body speaks the same language as our words (our commands). It is crucial to rise to the next level of dog training: **Behavior Training**.

More of this 'helicopter view' on Behavior Training you can find here: mygermanshepherd.org/periodical/advanced-dog-training-behavior-training

And the requirements of each dog training approach you can find here: mygermanshepherd.org/periodical/requirements-of-dog-training-approaches/

With a behavior-trained dog we simply *behave* - and the dog knows how we want him or her to behave! Without having to give many commands at all, not even many visual cues. *Now* we have risen to the summit of dog training: **Relationship Building**. Now our dog is our soulmate, (s)he knows exactly what we want, without us saying anything. Like in a mature human-human relationship (say with your partner).

Such a dog, your soulmate, you will never want to give up on. Such a dog will never end up in a shelter or high-kill kennel!

This, in a nutshell, is <u>why you need this book</u> - if you love your dog (see the book title!): It ensures that your love will continue through tomorrow - until your dog's last day.

Unlike all the puppy training techniques that ultimately are based on Obedience Training (even if the word isn't used), our proprietary dog and puppy training approach is <u>not</u> based on obedience.

Our **NO-Force, NO-Fear, NO-Fuss Puppy Training** is based on building the <u>right relationship</u> with our domesticated dogs. We use our own behavior to motivate our dogs to behave the way we want:

Show - Don't Tell

Accordingly, we never use any punishment at all, because that would undermine the loving relationship we want to have with our dogs.

We do use rewards, but *not* food treats. We treat our dogs in our family pack as they would be treated in their dog pack too.

And foremost, we accept them and appreciate them as what they are: an animal, but with a specifically and substantially modified genetical heritage - after a total of up to 33,000 years of targeted breeding!

Let me add one note: Initially (upon 'flying over it' rather than reading/studying it), our NO-Force, NO-Fear, NO-Fuss Puppy Training may *seem* 'impossible'. Recently a reader communicated her disbelief. Not in an email to me, but straight in her public review of the book!

She publicly *ridiculed* our puppy and dog training approach, arguing that she as a "retired vet tech" (mark that!) *knows* that dogs cannot be trained without some form of force, or raising fear, or at least using loads of food bribes. Sadly, readers like these are never available for a discussion: They don't dare to leave their email.

If *you* feel that our puppy and dog training approach presented in this book is 'impossible', and to get convinced of its success you would need to *see* it applied (instead of just reading it), then you can *watch* it being applied: Live. In over a hundred videos!

Because our favorite *professional* dog trainer Dan Abdelnoor (mygermanshepherd.org/go/online-dog-trainer) has built a massive video website that includes countless *live* dog training situations from when he visits his clients. You will see that he too uses NO Force and NO Fear (and very little food treats).

Thus, if my book cannot convince you of the success of our puppy and dog training approach, he can: mygermanshepherd.org/go/online-dog-trainer

Oh, and if you see the retired vet tech, kindly let her know too ;-)

Getting a Puppy

Getting a puppy is among the most wonderful moments in anyone's life. The anticipation, the prickling, bringing home a new puppy, seeing the pup playing with its toys, watching and influencing puppy development - all an outright amazing time to experience.

Then of course there come the puppy problems, certainly for most dog owners. And then comes aging - for our dog much quicker than for ourselves.

This is where this Puppy Development Guide can help. Nursing the right mindset to develop the puppy and keep the dog we wanted in the first place.

Indeed, the right puppy training is very much a two-way road. We should lead by example, and learn more ourselves than we require from our puppy to learn. Makes sense, really. We are human, the 'top animal', so we should be able to learn more.

The **right mindset** will allow us to benefit from a unique puppy training approach: Puppy Training without applying any force, without raising any fear, and without bribe (that's what food treats really are). Also, without shouting or scolding, and without pulling on the collar or lead, or pushing the puppy. No, no fuss at all!

That's why we call this The NO-Force, NO-Fear, NO-Fuss Puppy Training.

A completely gentle and relaxed puppy training. Surprisingly, it's the most effective dog training nonetheless. I have yet to see a puppy trainer or dog trainer who teaches a dog the desired behavior in less time and with less effort - and then gets consistent results.

But let's be clear about this: The 'desired behavior' is a human interpretation of the behavior of an animal.

More so, I have witnessed time and time again that often dog owners demand a certain behavior from their puppy just because they are stressed themselves, or in bad mood, or more generally, the 'bossy' type of person.

And then, the next moment or the next day, the same situation again, but this time they demand a *different* behavior from their puppy - because they are in a *different* mood.

For a dog, and much more for a small puppy, such *inconsistency* is the worst 'training', because it confuses the pup, and confusion means stress to a dog, whether young dog or old dog. Not as much stress as a pig experiences, but considerably more stress than the average human feels in such situations.

We must avoid this stress for our pup - because:

Stress results in behavior problems

That's why I'd like to encourage you to adopt the right mindset before you adopt a puppy, and then each time before you engage with the pup - and particularly during dedicated training sessions.

The right mindset we can only develop when we better understand the human-canine relationship. Therefore, in this book I will also share with you what I currently call the PRIME SECRET about dogs.

This is about a discovery that I made only after studying canines, while observing dog behavior with the extent of inquisitiveness that scientists share with children. One of those rare streaks of luck maybe.

This discovery hasn't yet been published in any mainstream media, and certainly none of the famous dog trainers shares this insight yet, or they would have aggressively marketed it - since anything relating to training puppies and dog training is their business.

So, is this 'prime secret' maybe far-fetched? Certainly not. It is one of those secrets that seem *obvious* - once we got a hint.

You will see in a moment yourself, this Prime Secret makes sense; so much that it just *has to* be correct.

In the remaining chapters of this book we will then make use of this 'prime secret' to develop a *completely gentle and relaxed* puppy training approach that we can apply straight away to our own puppies:

The NO-Force, NO-Fear, NO-Fuss Puppy Training

Note that although the term 'puppy' is associated with dogs of a young age (typically until about 9 to 12 months of age physically, and until about 24 to 30 months of age mentally - depending on breed), actually in many regards even an old dog may show typical symptoms of a pup, namely when the dog is placed into a new home.

Meaning, despite being titled 'Puppy Development Guide and Puppy 101', this book's guidance indeed also proves helpful if you have for example a rescue dog of say 6 years of age!

So, don't be put off by the term puppy: You can very well apply the specific training approach presented in this book to old dogs as well.

Nonetheless, after a few months you may want to get another guide that specifically addresses adult dogs and their behavior. That book should then be the complete House Training Guide: House Training

Dogs to Behave Well in a High Value Home (mygermanshepherd.org/go/house-training-guide).

Because **house training** (not housebreaking!) is the *major* part of all dog training - and 'high value home' doesn't necessarily mean financially, but emotionally: You don't want that your dog destroys the house when you give the dog free run of the house while you are away!

Where to Get a Puppy

It is not the focus of this book to delve into detail about where to buy a puppy. However, knowing the essentials may help to develop the **right mindset** - which is the overall purpose of this book.

So, please find below some explanations of the various market places to get a puppy or dog.

Backyard Breeders

This is how most people get their puppy: They search classifieds (advertisements), and the vast majority of all puppy classifieds are from backyard breeders (byb).

Advertisements from ordinary owners of a female dog (dam) that got puppies. Either coincidentally, or because the dog owners planned it that way, seeking to make a profit from selling the puppies - this again is the majority of puppy classifieds.

Backyard breeders typically have not planned what to breed, i.e.:

- which dam should mate with which sire
- and for what reasons
- in order to get what kind of offspring?

In particular, backyard breeders don't have the means to *choose* their breeding stock, they simply go with what they have or what they find on the street (quite literally) - without making an investment to get the *right* dam and sire mate.

This is *not always* bad:

- You may be lucky and find a healthy and well looked-after small breed dog at a backyard breeder if you know how to sort out the lemons before you decide on a dog (backyard breeders know this, hence many will try to make you feel attached to one of their pups early on).

- Cross-breeding (of the *right* dogs) actually has health benefits. Note that it is the incredible extent of *inbreeding* of irresponsible breeders that has led to the proliferation of hereditary diseases of the most popular dog breeds. With a *cross-breed* (mix or mutt) you are less likely to buy into these diseases (and thus to exacerbate them further!)

Our site members from Australia report that there, backyard breeders have healthier(!) dogs than professional purebred breeders - while for USA, UK, Germany, Spain, and Portugal I know that you would need immense *luck* to get a healthy *purebred* dog from a backyard breeder. With a *cross-breed* your chances are always better, see above.

Pet Stores

In most states, this is the number two place for people to get a puppy. A local or regional pet store that sells all kinds of dog equipment, as well as small puppies.

Pet store dogs are almost always supplied by Puppy Mill Breeders (see next), and the reason is simple: The pet store needs to make a decent profit to fund the store.

Despite being a costly brick-and-mortar business, they have to keep the sales price low in order to sell the puppies at all.

With the sales price being limited to the low end, a pet store can only realize a profit if they buy their stock cheap. *Very* cheap. Between $20 for a sought-after purebreed to *nothing* for a wimpy-looking small mix (as a deal-sweetener or, more often, to establish a new business relationship).

Puppy Mill Breeders

That's where the puppy mill breeders help out. They are willing to sell their dogs cheap. *Dirt* cheap.

In fact, they know they cannot realize higher prices anyway, since their dogs are not well looked after and healthy, but rather carry hereditary diseases and infections caught on the premises of the puppy mill. Also, the pups have not been socialized when they left their mum and litter mates.

However, puppy mill breeders too need to make a profit! Knowing they won't get much for their puppies when they sell them to the pet stores, the only variable they can influence is the cost of the breeding dogs and their offspring.

The biggest cost factors are vet bills and spending time with the dogs and with the puppies. Hence puppy mill breeders save on health screenings and health treatment of their breeding dogs (dam and sire) as well as their puppies, and they cannot afford to spend time on the socialisation process of the puppies either.

For the same reason, it just doesn't make sense for puppy mill breeders to retire a breeding dog *just because* it has obvious health issues. Instead, they have a strong economic desire to continue to use breeding stock that has already been *clearly identified* as <u>unsuitable</u> for breeding healthy puppies!

Purebred Breeders

If you want to get a puppy of a certain breed, purebred breeders is where to look.

Yes, these puppies do cost more, but on the other hand, having to cope with puppy behavior problems, adult dog problems, and high vet bills for life costs *much* more - both money and nerves!

Purebred breeders know that they can command a decent sales price for superb puppies, but not for a puppy that is unhealthy from the start or has obvious behavior issues.

This gives the purebred breeders more playing field as regards the cost (selecting top breeding stock, paying for regular vet checks, providing excellent food, and spending much time with each puppy). And it motivates most purebred breeders to only use and breed quality dogs.

Also, most purebred breeders focus on one breed only - out of passion. They have a personal motivation to maintain a high quality of breeding stock of their chosen breed. This motivation may even be bigger than that to make a profit from selling puppies.

'Profit' in apostrophes because once you consider the time spent to care for each pup over the first seven or more weeks, there isn't a profit to make from dog breeding anyway. Many would find that they can better monetize their time another way if they just gave it some thought.

This is crucial to understand: It explains why it generally is so *unlikely* to get a healthy *and* well looked-after puppy at a bargain price (ie primarily from backyard breeders (p31), but also from some dubious professional purebred breeders).

Dog Shelters and Breed Rescue Centers

Finally, dog shelters and breed rescue centers are a completely different story. Obviously, the majority here are older dogs, not puppies. However, you may be surprised how many small puppies you can choose from when you visit several shelters or rescue centers.

Be it that the dam was pregnant before it came to the shelter, or because people abandon puppies for any of a number of reasons. For example:

- too many puppies in one litter
- puppies grow too quickly
- puppies make a mess (they do!)
- puppies require too much time (a LOT!)
- food and vet cost (easily $250 in first 6 weeks)
- dogs not allowed in apartment
- lost job
- had to move house
- etc.

It's important to understand that in the majority of cases puppies as well as older dogs(!) are not abandoned to shelters because of health issues or behavior issues, but purely because of owner issues (see the reasons above).

The great advantage of getting a dog from a rescue center or shelter is that these dogs:

- have undergone a full health-check
- are temperament-tested
- and are already spayed or neutered.

In case of older dogs, further benefits are that:

- they are typically fully house-trained
- well-socialized
- and much more reliable and peaceful and quieter than puppies.

Whether you train them or not, older rescue dogs typically won't chew your Gucci shoes or pee on your Persian rug - while a puppy almost certainly will at some point.

Indeed, it is much more likely that you get a healthy puppy or older dog from breed rescue centers and dog shelters than that you get a healthy puppy from a pet store.

Also note that - contrary to pet stores, puppy mill breeders, and backyard breeders - dog shelters and rescue centers do not have the financial motivation to sell a dog to you at all. They will rather check if they can 'sell' you to the dog in question. Meaning, they try to *match* dog and prospective owner - to ensure that the dog does not have to suffer the shelter experience again.

Shelters *want* to place each dog in the right hands. All others (maybe except some reputable purebred breeders) primarily want your money. Yes.

What Do I Need for a New Puppy?

Before we bring our new puppy home, we need to make certain puppy preparations:

- How to puppy-proof your house
- Prepare a place to rest and sleep
- Prepare a place to eat and drink
- Puppy Safekeeping
- Puppy Grooming
- Get a variety of quality toys

With these puppy preparations in place we will be well prepared, so that we can keep calm when we interact with our pup - which is a prerequisite to avoid puppy training mistakes.

How to Puppy-Proof Your House

- **Prevent electrical shock** when our pup's paw reaches into an electrical socket: These top outlet plug covers will help: mygermanshepherd .org/go/outlet-plug-cover

- **Prevent falling down stairs or getting through where it shouldn't** while our puppy is still unadept or dangerously playful: This super sturdy bamboo gate helps (mygermanshepherd .org/go/bamboo-gate), but we need to raise it to about 80% of our pup's chestsize perimeter (mygermanshepherd.org/how-to-measure-your-dogs-height-and-weight - Yes, *and* chestsize perimeter *and* front leg length, but the link would have become too long ;-)

- A good alternative can be this steel safety gate (mygermanshepherd.org/go/safety-gate), but we must tighten the pressure mount *a lot*, and even then a strong puppy may be able to push the mount out of its anchor!)

- While our pup is very small (depending on breed even with an adult dog) we may also want to consider a strong banister shield (mygermansh epherd.org/go/banister-shield). In such case, we better get one which is *clear* so that our pup can look through and relax (opaque ones can increase aggression).

- **Protect our pup from sharp edges** with these impact absorbing foam corner guards: mygerma nshepherd.org/go/foam-corner-guards

- **Protect our pup from electrical wires and any type of cords** that it might chew on, get entangled, or even strangled. Wire hiders (mygerm anshepherd.org/go/wire-hider) and cord mates (mygermanshepherd.org/go/cord-mate) can help here.

- **Lock away all household detergents, knives, grapes, high-sugar and high-fat foods etc**. Even small puppies often can find ways to say jump on the kitchen counter, or open cupboards with mouth or paws, or open doors. The general rule is: What isn't locked is accessable! The most hilarious video I've seen of a dog 'going wild' is this: mygermanshepherd.org/dog-kitchen-count er-surfing-extreme :-)

Prepare a Place to Rest and Sleep

It is crucial that we get a comfortable resting place (mygermanshepherd.org/go/westpaw-nap-blanket) for our puppy for *every* room where we want our dog to be close to us.

Else our pup will restlessly seek a place *near us* where (s)he is comfortable *and* where we let the pup lie down without commanding all the time (or inviting to jump on our lap or whatever). Such restlessness would quickly lead to stress for a dog, and stress leads to behavior and health issues. This is *why* we need to provide a comfortable resting place in *every* room where we want our dog to be close to us.

A cheaper alternative is this pet bed (mygermanshepherd.org/go/bolster-pet-bed).

Obviously this should be a comfortable place for our puppy: Sore elbows is a common ailment of dogs that are confined to lie on hard grounds. This, and the associated vet cost, can easily be avoided by providing the *right* resting place like shown above.

In addition, for a good night's sleep we must get a suitable crate, and put it in a place where there's no draft or radiator heat, and no electrical wiring.

Ideally we place the crate where our pup can somewhat observe what's going on in the family (namely its Pack), while still having a chance to freely retreat to a quieter place (particularly important for times when feeling unwell).

An annex to the living room or a room corner is a great place for the dog crate. Make sure that there is no draft, no immediate radiator heat, and no wiring from electrical items like fridges etc.

It does *not* make sense to put the crate in our own bedroom - unless we stay most of the day in bed. And it is certainly a bad idea to move the crate around. No, decide on a suitable place, and leave it there.

Note that if the crate is in a separate room (where we are not), always leave the door a bit open so that you don't cut off your pup's hereditary quest to be close to its Pack, and that it doesn't feel lonely or anxious either. This is all the more important while you have a puppy, but it is relevant at every age in order to keep your dog calm and healthy.

Please don't get one of those metal cage crates (mygermanshepherd.org/go/metal-cage-crate), which are surprisingly popular.

Most dog owners who get such kennel-style cages for their puppy and/or adult dog are worried about potty accidents, or that the dog may be making a mess of the house otherwise.

However, both are a matter of training, and as such easily avoidable if we provide the *right* training to our puppy - like you find it here in this book.

Then there will be no need to lock away our pup and put it behind bars!

Indeed, commercial crates are neither necessary nor the most appropriate for our pup's needs. Why?

Almost all commercial crates have a roof, and some vendors even argue that puppies want this, that's why they would crawl under cupboards etc.

But no, a dog is not a rabbit that seeks to hide in a burrow. During night time when our pup wants to sleep it needs to feel safe. Dogs in the wild don't choose a den with a roof either; instead what they do seek is a den where they can hide from prying eyes while they are asleep - but with a quick exit path in case of danger!

This instinctive desire develops instantly when puppies are left without litter mates and mother - which is the case at the time we get our puppy - if we get the pup from a reputable breeder, dog shelter or breed rescue center.

Also, a suitable puppy crate is one where our pup can access a bowl of fresh water nearby, without risking to wet its blanket.

In addition, the crate must be of sufficient size for our pup to *fully stretch out*, and of course to stand up - regardless how fast it is growing. Needless to say, the crate should be made of natural material and have no sharp edges.

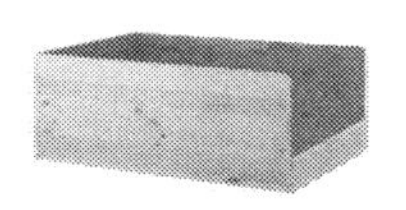

Therefore, a suitable puppy crate is one that you can simply build yourself by putting together a few pieces of wood, like you see in this example (taken from our Periodical Building a Den for your Dog at mygermanshepherd.org/periodical/building-a-den-for-your-dog).

Note that there is no need to change the crate in line with your pup's growth. Just build the right one straight away. What we put *inside* the crate will allow our puppy to feel comfortable regardless of initial crate size:

Put another cushioned dog mat (mygermanshepherd.org/go/westpaw-nap-blanket) plus a quality blanket (mygermanshepherd.org/go/westpaw-dog-blanket) inside, a drinking bowl (mygermanshepherd.org/go/spill-proof-dog-travel-bowl) next to it, and that's it!

Prepare a Place to Eat and Drink

Our puppy needs a bowl of fresh water very close to its crate.

A fantastic drinking bowl (mygermanshepherd.org/go/spill-proof-dog-travel-bowl) comes from Jolly Pets, and it has the added benefit to be spill-proof, so it is also perfect when we are traveling with our puppy.

Don't think "No water at night, or we get potty accidents and late-night potty walks!".

No, permanent access to fresh water is a MUST when we have a puppy. Also, its just a question of two or three nights, and then normally puppies have figured out that excessive drinking at night puts pressure on their bladder - which no dog can bear!

Note that a dog's bladder is much more susceptible to bladder infections than the human bladder: mygermanshepherd.org/my-german-shepherd/german-shepherd-health/german-shepherd-bladder-infection

Note that all linked content is relevant to your puppy regardless of breed or mix - *unless* I write in one of the linked Periodicals that a certain point is breed-specific.

Another important point here is that, from the outset, our puppy should learn to eat slowly, not gulping down the food - which sooner or later may lead to Vomiting (mygermanshepherd.org/my-german-shepherd/german-shepherd-health/german-shepherd-vomiting), Diarrhea (mygermanshepherd.org/my-german-shepherd/german-shepherd-health/german-shepherd-diarrhea), Bloat or Gastric Torsion (mygermanshepherd.org/my-german-shepherd/german-shepherd-health/german-shepherd-bloat-or-gastric-torsion), and even Gastroenteritis or Pancreatitis (mygermanshepherd.org/my-german-shepherd/german-shepherd-health/german-shepherd-bloat-or-gastric-torsion).

A great **eat-slow training** is to give our pup an eat-slow bowl that fulfils its promise (most such bowls don't).

The best bowl on the market that really enforces our puppy to eat slowly - without the annoyance and mess of skidding all over the place - is the eat-slow bowl from Greedy Pup (mygermanshepherd.org/go/eat-slow-bowl). However it's synthetic (polypropeline) which isn't the ideal material to eat from.

The same is true for this much cheaper alternative - but this one doesn't stay put: mygermanshepherd.org/go/eat-slow-bowl-third-best

The best stainless steel eat-slow bowl is this one (yet even cheaper!): mygermanshepherd.org /go/eat-slow-bowl-metal

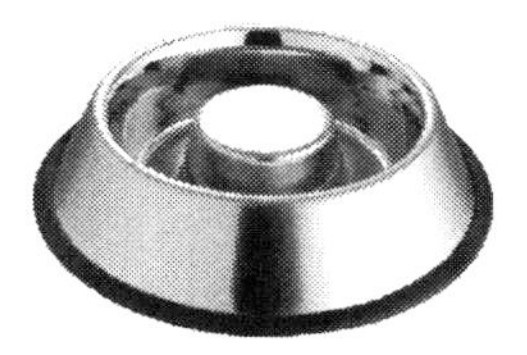

However, for small puppies with a short tongue the lug in the middle may be too high.

Important: Place one drinking bowl very close to the crate, and another drinking bowl together with the eat-slow-bowl where you would like your pup to eat (whether kitchen, garden, or wherever).

But move these two bowls about 50 inches to 2 meters apart so that spilled slobber and food does not get into the drinking water.

Needless to say, we must clean all bowls before every meal, and particularly well any bowl that is outside - because these become a gathering place for all sorts of microbes and micro-critters within a mere hours.

While some dog breeds have an excellent antibacterial oral microflora and stomach enzymes - in order to cope with their scavenging (mygermanshepherd.org/periodical/how-to-stop-scavenging), especially the toy breeds have not; hence these require an even stricter hygiene.

Puppy Safekeeping

The basic necessities are:

A reflective safety dog collar (mygermanshepherd.org/go/rogz-reflective-dog-collar), together with...

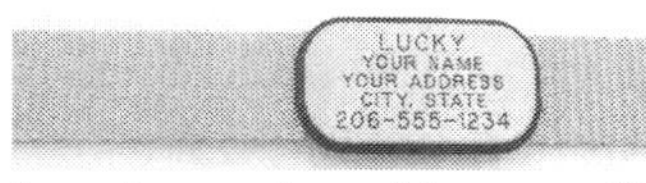

...a flat-attaching, non-come-off ID tag: mygermanshepherd.org/go/dog-collar-tag

Note that for example in the USA alone (where figures are readily available), in an average year about 10 million(!) *pets* are lost (more than 5% annually), and less than 25 percent of those pets are reunited with their human families!

Also note that the above reflective collar is merely for outdoors/dog walking. While indoors, and particularly at night, a soft padded genuine leather collar is *much* better. No other material or type of collar can compete with the feel-good factor a soft padded genuine leather collar provides.

You *will* notice the difference: How much more *relaxed* your puppy is the next morning when you let it sleep with the leather collar. But do leave on the leather collar, even at night. This is necessary both for safety and behavior purposes (see later Collar Freeze and Isolation).

This is the bestselling soft padded genuine leather collar (available in various sizes): mygermanshepherd.org/go/bestselling-leather-collar

A short lead (mygermanshepherd.org/go/teaching-lead) - This image shows the teaching lead from Sarah Hodgson which is perfect for puppies too (unless you have a small breed dog, then this leash is too heavy), so you can buy just *one* short leash and have it for life.

A long line (mygermanshepherd.org/go/long-line) - indispensable for safety and training purposes (see later).

Finally, of course we need a **comprehensive first aid kit** formulated for canines.

You may want to go for a good commercial kit (mygermanshepherd.org/go/pet-first-aid-kit), but note that none of them holds all the items that we will need for our puppy - sooner or later!

So, here's a quick list what our customized puppy first aid kit should comprise, in addition to commercial kits like the one above:

- Vetericyn Wound and Infection Spray: mygermanshepherd.org/go/vetericyn-wound-and-infection-spray
- Vetericyn Eye Wash: mygermanshepherd.org/go /vetericyn-eye-wash
- Zymox Otic Ear Treatment *Without(!)* Hydrocortisone (to understand *why* see later): mygermanshepherd.org/go/ear-treatment-without-cortisone
- Paw Protection Cream: mygermanshepherd.org/go/mushers-secret
- Flexible hard bandage: mygermanshepherd.org/go/hard-bandage
- Liquid (soft) bandage: mygermanshepherd.org/go/soft-bandage
- Styptic powder to stop bleeding: mygermanshepherd.org/go/styptic-powder
- Canine pain relief: mygermanshepherd.org/go/canine-pain-relief

Puppy Grooming

We need:

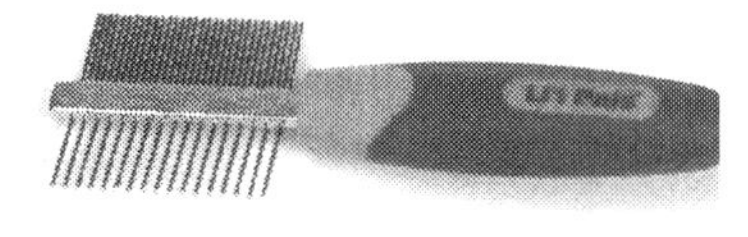

A small comb: mygermanshepherd.org /go/comb-small

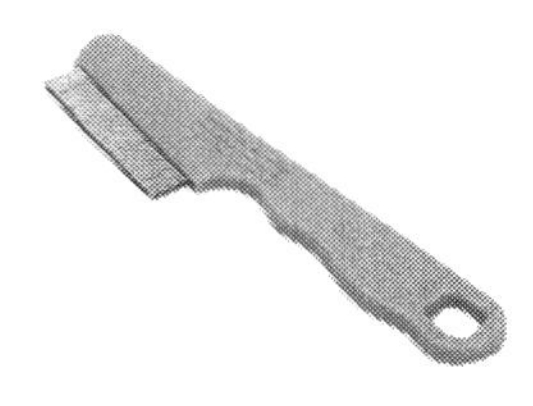

A flea comb: mygermanshep herd.org/go/flea-comb

And a furminator to tackle shedding: mygermanshepherd. org/go/furminator

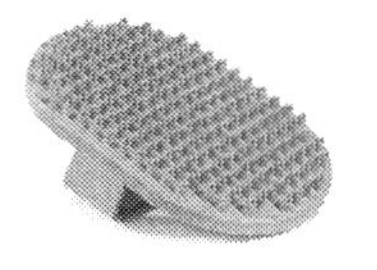

A pin-headed rubber brush to wash our puppy, to massage the skin and to improve blood circulation and oil distribution, and for bonding: myger manshepherd.org/go/rubber-brush

Although, there is a newer remedy which is perfect for bonding (and basic grooming):

The love glove: mygermanshepherd.org/go/love-glove

Zymox' antibacterial and antifungal pet rinse (mygermanshepherd.org/go/antibacterial-antifungal-pet-rinse) to restore the health of our pup's skin...

... while bathing it in a bath tub suitable for puppies: mygerman shepherd.org/go/pup-tub

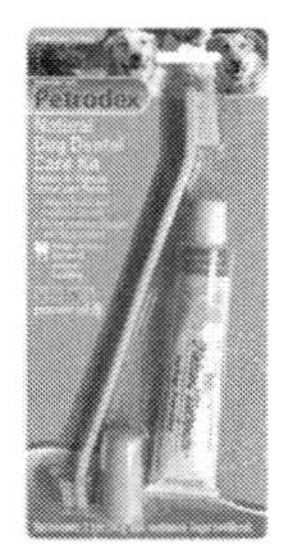

A dental care kit (long brush, finger brush, and pet-safe/swallowable dog toothpaste): mygermanshepherd.org/go/dog-dental-care-kit

Get a Variety of Quality Toys

Puppies need A LOT of attention. Indeed, almost non-stop attention while they are not sleeping.

Thankfully though, puppies sleep LONG and A LOT too, in order to be able to physically cope with their impressive growth rate (at times pups will sleep 18 to 20 hours a day).

With attention during our pup's awake hours I don't even mean so much that they are safe, I mean attention so that they don't get bored:

The majority of dog behavior problems result from boredom in dogs!

Of course, we cannot be with our pup 24*7, minus sleep time. But to a certain extent we can get our pup pretty occupied with playing on its own (but close to us so that, with a glimpse, we can observe what's happening).

For this to happen, we need to provide our puppy with a variety of quality puppy toys.

Requirements of Quality Puppy Toys

- Our pup must LOVE to play with it (we need to find out)
- SAFE for our pup
- USEFUL for Education and Training
- Mentally and physically STIMULATING
- NON-TOXIC
- DURABLE
- and EASY TO CLEAN

A lot of requirements, yes!

Variety of Puppy Toys

With variety of puppy toys I mean that we should provide at least one toy from each toy category:

- Chew Toys
- Activity Toys
- Treat Toys
- Squeaky Toys
- Puzzle Toys
- Tug Toys

Apart from pure chew toys, all dog toys can be considered interactivity toys, as they either return sound, light, or movement when our pup plays with them. This is great, because it helps to prevent boredom.

Of course, every puppy has different preferences (and these change with our pup's age). Nonetheless, here's a list of our overall winners in each toy category:

- **Chew Toys**: Westpaw's Hurley (mygermanshepherd.org/go/dog-chew-toys-hurley) is a super-tough, multi-functional chew bone that's also ideal to be taken outside - it even floats on the water!

- **Activity Toys**: Chuckit! (mygermanshepherd.org/go/dog-activity-toys-chuckit-ball) is a non-toxic high-impact ball that's made to last, and this ball is much more fun for our pup than the typical ball it may discover in our household.

- **Treat Toys**: Westpaw's Tux (mygermanshepherd.org/go/dog-treat-toys-tux) is a great example. It's made of a non-toxic material trading as Zogoflex. Tux is pliable, bouncing, recyclable, buoyant, and dishwasher-safe too. If you have a puppy that has no retrieval instinct in its genes, then try this toy - your pup will run after it, just to retrieve the treat you put inside!

- **Squeaky Toys**: Hartz Roundabouts (mygermanshepherd.org/go/dog-squeaky-toys-hartz-roundabouts) is one of the very few examples of squeak-only toys. They are made of latex that lasts. Note though that squeaky toys don't make every puppy happy (and certainly not every owner either). Some (puppies/owners) find the noises disturbing or annoying. But it's worth to try out one of these toys as well.

- **Puzzle Toys**: Hide-a-Squirrel (mygermanshepherd.org/go/dog-puzzle-toys-hide-a-squirrel) is an immensely popular multi-functional toy that promises our puppy loads of lasting fun, as well as mental and physical stimulation. But note that, because of the small parts, we MUST constantly observe our pup with these toys - even if it figured out how to play alone with them. Best really is to always use these toys as bonding time with your pup.

- **Tug Toys**: Most Tug Toys perform poorly, and it's better to just take a strong leather lead or cotton rope. However, one toy that isn't actually promoted as Tug Toy does have its merits: Fresh-N-Floss (mygermanshepherd.org/go/dog-tug-toys-fresh-n-floss) is tough enough for a short, quick pull with our puppy, and while doing so it is proven to be brilliant on our dog's teeth - while gentle enough for its gums.

Overall A LOT of puppy preparations we have to make, oh yes!

The Right Mindset

Once we have made all the above puppy preparations, we know that we are well-prepared - so we can *relax*.

This is crucial in order to be able to apply our gentle and relaxed puppy training approach. Because:

Our own energy state transfers to our pup!

Whether we are stressed or calm, sad or happy, pleased or upset - our own energy state substantially impacts on our puppy's behavior, and hence on our chances to raise the dog we want.

Every puppy has an inherited unlimited desire to *please* us, to become the dog we want (very different to our children who, to a large degree, become like we are). This is the result of up to 33,000 years of targeted breeding of canines to become our modern domesticated dogs, that we share our life with, and our house.

Consider that for most of this time, we can reliably assume that there was on average one new dog generation a year - unlike with humans, where a new generation has always required 20 or more years on average. Thus, our modern dogs have been shaped for about 33,000 generations - this is *more* than we, the homo sapiens, have been shaped!

This is why our domesticated dogs are *so much* unlike wolves, their distant ancestors - who would try to kill us in an instant, would they share the house (and often the bed) with us like our dogs do. And *this* is why our domesticated dogs are so much like ourselves, mentally and emotionally so *close* to us. Amazing!

But this is also the reason why our dogs are so receptive for our emotions and *how* we behave. And this is why we need to be calm with our puppy, and not transfer our stress onto our dog. To help our pup understand what we want, we need nothing but to provide at least basic care and the *right* training.

While *we* choose who we want to live with (spouse, friend, pet,...), our puppy did not choose - yet loves us nonetheless. But it takes time to understand what we want - like it takes time in a human partnership too. So <u>we must be patient</u>, and <u>improve our own training approach</u>, instead of scolding our puppy, or giving up on our dog. Okay?

Always remember:

Dogs are energy recipients

This means, dogs rapidly assume our own energy state (unlike cats, which are energy donors). Thus, if we have a stressed, aggressive dog - we should first look at our own behavior, and consider if maybe we are often engaging with our dog when we are stressed. Then it's no surprise if our dog becomes aggressive after a while - because for dogs, stress quickly leads to aggression (and for many humans too).

Bringing Home a New Puppy

Introducing a new puppy into our life, our family, brings a major change - regardless how many dogs we've had before, and regardless how many other animals we live with.

Because, every puppy is in one way or another *different* to other puppies. And every adult dog is in one way or another different to other adult dogs. Even among the same breed, oh yes.

It is these finer differences that can make or break the dog-human relationship. These reasons come on top of the more well-known reasons (grousepup.hubpages.com/hub/Why-So-Many-Dogs-End-Up-At-A-Shelter-Or-The-Pound) why so many of the yesterday-beloved puppies today or tomorrow end up at the animal shelter, dog pound or breed rescue center, or being medically euthanized or silently killed in the backyard, or maltreated!

If this book, besides presenting our NO-Force, NO-Fear, NO-Fuss Puppy Training, can convince just one of today's puppy owners to hold on to their dog tomorrow - then I'd consider this as a great start for the much needed change in society.

The *right* training can do this magic, because it ensures that we get the dog we want - and such a dog, we just don't want to lose!

Puppy Development Timeline

Here we don't want to discuss all that happens (or is supposed to happen) during the different puppy development stages - there are already enough sources that merely *describe* the puppy stages.

Instead, here we will focus on those aspects of puppy development that we need to understand in order to successfully apply our unique puppy training approach: The NO-Force, NO-Fear, NO-Fuss Puppy Training.

Canine puppies of course develop continually anyway, and any consideration of puppy development stages is a human interpretation. Nonetheless, it seems to help our own understanding of the right puppy training when we split up the puppy development timeline into different puppy stages:

Litter Socialization

This period lasts from birth until about age 7 or 8 weeks (depending on breed).

During the first 7 to 8 weeks, mum and litter mates play a crucial role for the development of each puppy. Most importantly, through the interaction with mum and litter mates:

1. each pup learns that it is *not the only one* or the most important living being
2. each pup learns when enough is enough
3. and each pup learns to use its mouth responsibly

When a puppy gets too carried away with any behavior, mum - and later litter mates too - will stop it. For example, when a pup playfully nips mum or mates, and they find it's getting too much, their typical response is either a high-pitched yelp or a short pinch in the ruff of the pup's neck, and then totally *ignoring* the pup, or immediately ignoring the pup for a moment - before play may continue.

As the name suggests, a puppy should not be removed from its animal pack during the **Litter Socialization** period. The dad however (or sire) does not play any significant role among the modern domesticated dog packs (but does so among wild dogs).

Family Socialization

This period typically lasts from about age 7 or 8 weeks (when the puppy is taken away from the litter) until around age 3 months (depending on breed), so merely 4 weeks!

Around week 8 is the right time for a puppy to be given to its ultimate human family pack. By now the pup normally will have had sufficient litter socialization, will have received one or even two rounds of vaccinations (at least if from a responsible breeder or from a shelter; see the chapter 'Where to get a Puppy', p~30), and the puppy is safe to interact with humans and other dogs, and to be taken outside, without infecting us or other animals, or be infected by us or other animals (for more detail see Puppy Vaccination, p~72).

These four weeks of **Family Socialization** are critical in terms of 'getting the dog we want': We must intensely **socialize** our new puppy and systematically expose it to a broad variety of noises, sights, smells, animals, humans, and situations, so that our pup will not fear any of these in the future (see later How to Best Socialize a Puppy, p~150).

Indeed fear is the underlying cause of the majority of dog aggression and other behavior problems later in the dog's life, and hence in our life.

For this reason, the key point to observe during the Family Socialization period is that we avoid all situations that might make our dog overly fearful.

In other words, we must already demonstrate our Pack leadership at a time where most new puppy owners get carried away with how cute the pup is: We spoil the puppy with attention, foods, toys and play to an extent its mum and litter mates would never do! And, we 'comfort' the puppy with loads of 'sentimental praise' upon the slightest indication of fear - which to a dog sounds like we are worried too (to understand this, see the Dog Training Toolkit: mygermanshepherd.org/go/dog-training-toolkit).

Contrary to what the puppy learned from its *dog pack* during Litter Socialization, now during **Family Socialization** the pup learns from us (its *family pack*) that it is the most important living being, or the *only* puppy. Quite literally actually in most dog owner households.

This creates a multitude of problems, to which we will get in just a moment.

Puberty

This period lasts from around 3 months of age until around 6 months of age (depending on breed).

Like with children, this is the time when puppies make us most stress and distress. They will test our consistency and persistence - certainly de facto, and I would argue it's consciously: They *want* to find out how far they can go, what they can do.

Puppies don't want to be scolded, but they want to know what our reaction in each situation is.

Pups want to know which place they have in their Pack!

Note the pup's development between these two puppy stages: During Family Socialization, typically puppies will appreciate that we demonstrate our Pack leadership, but starting with puberty, puppies will intensely test their Pack position (some breeds sooner than others).

This is a genetic canine quest, and it will not stop before dogs reach the (breed-specific) turning point from adult dog to senior dog!

Once again, during most part of a dog's life, *every* dog will follow its genetic quest and frequently test its Pack position (unless the dog is traumatized).

This is one of the dog traits that has been carried over from wild dogs to domesticated dogs - despite 4,000 years or more of *specialized* dog breeding. - Maybe breeders didn't target this trait, who knows.

Quite remarkable, really. Particularly when we consider how many problems dog owners around the world have that result from their dog's pursuit of Pack leadership!

If I were a dog breeder, *this* is the dog trait I would probably have focused on first with the breed selection. Maybe breeders did, but failed - we don't know.

Adolescence

This is the final period we want to look at here. It lasts from about age 6 months until 9 to 12 months of age (depending on breed).

This is the time where all the prior (litter and family) socialization and pack positioning either pays off or, where we may be facing despair!

These older puppies now want to explore their surroundings and they seek adventures. This coincides with gaining their final height and strength, as well as actively seeking out other dogs to mate - unless spayed/neutered (mygermanshepherd.org/periodical/gsd-spaying-and-neutering).

Our puppy will still gain size thereafter (fill out) - until at least 24 or 30 months of age (depending on breed and feeding of course) - but in terms of height, that's it.

Depending on its behavior (which in turn depends on our training!), we may soon no longer consider ourselves as puppy owners but as dog owners, and our puppy soon *looks* like an adult dog too.

So, this whole puppy development takes no more than one year!

However, this was all about how puppies develop. More important for our NO-Force, NO-Fear, NO-Fuss Puppy Training is how we influence this development. In other words, how *we* develop our puppy, and how *we* develop the bonding or relationship *with* our puppy.

These aspects will become more obvious as we progress.

Puppy Vaccination

As mentioned under Family Socialization (p~66), by the time most people get their puppy (around 8 weeks of age) the pup will normally have received its first one or two vaccinations if acquired from a reputable breeder or shelter.

Note though that there are **conflicting views** on vaccinations (like with everything really). The extremes:

- Some (typically *older*, not up-to-date) veterinarians believe that sufficient puppy immunization does not take place before 4.5 months of age, and thus this would be the *earliest* time for puppies to be safely taken outside to public places and to interact with other dogs (ie be socialized).
- Some dog breeders, owners, and (typically *younger*, recently trained) veterinarians believe that the above view is unfounded - and many of them have successfully raised generations of dogs without any vaccinations at all, while letting the puppies explore public places and interact with other dogs from as early as 7 weeks of age!

Based on their own education and experience, both groups (and everyone in between these extremes) have good reasons for their beliefs.

What we should bear in mind though is that:

1. Canine vaccines have dramatically improved over time (similar to human vaccines, but less so). Immunization has become *much* quicker, and lasts *much* longer before a booster is required to maintain immunization - eg for rabies (even the *not* up-to-date) veterinarians now accept that a booster every 5 to 7 years is sufficient.

2. With many pathogens, incubation lengthened (the time from infection to symptom visibility and disease outbreak)

3. There is a BIG difference between life-threatening infections (life-threatening for the dog and/or for the human carer?), and controllable and curable infections (curable for the dog and/or for the human carer?)

4. The risk of infection (both with life-threatening and with curable pathogens) is very different depending on the geographical region (some pathogens are only endemic in certain geographies), *and* depending on the dog's individual living environment (some dogs are 95% indoors, others share life with children and/or other animals, others visit dog parks, and others live on a farm or freely roam the wilderness, etc)

5. An infection that doesn't kill *improves* the body's defenses and allows to thwart off future attacks, both of the same pathogen *and* of other pathogens

6. Obviously, *every* vaccination increases the likelihood for the dog to **develop autoimmune disorders**: The now widespread suffering of practically all dog breeds from allergies, digestive disorders, arthritis, cancer etc has been found to be strongly linked to over-vaccination, as well as to the blanket treatment with antibiotics and corticosteroids!

7. The current scientific view now is that only ONE vaccination for the endemic diseases should be undertaken (ie no future boosters), but LATER than it is still common practice, namely **at age 12 weeks**. This age has been identified to offer the greatest chance to *really* protect the puppy - while up until this age the pup's *maternal antibodies* (ingested with the mother's milk) are likely to *inactivate* the vaccine, and after this age they become too weak to fight off the actual pathogen.

8. Note however that the natural weakening of maternal antibodies *differs* immensely between different dogs (even of the same breed) and from one pathogen to another. Hence the vaccination at age 12 weeks gives the best immunization *overall*, but obviously not in each individual case (no different to the present vaccination practice!)

So, if you are worried about vaccinating your puppy only once and not before (and not after) age 12 weeks - and if you have the money to spend - you may want to consider to have titer tests done at the time(s) you - or your vet!? - want to vaccinate. The titers will show if that's *really* a good time at your pup's individual development stage (and if the vaccination is needed at all)!

No one, not even five different vets, can take this right and responsibility off you. You should make this educated decision yourself, after taking all views as well as local laws into account.

In case your local vet appears not up-to-date, you should of course consult another local vet. Nonetheless, it is helpful if you know of the typical basic immunization yourself, so here it is:

In many geographies the typical **basic immunization** is the multivalent vaccine DHLPPCv. In addition, rabies vaccination and lyme vaccine inoculation *where relevant.*

DHLPPCv is a six-pack vaccination combining:

- Distemper - a viral infection of the nervous system that can cause anything from gastrointestinal upset to pneumonia, seizures and tremors (no known cure!)

- Hepatitis - a viral infection of the liver that can cause acute liver failure

- Leptospirosis - a bacterial infection of liver and kidneys that can increase the chances of death 30 to 40 fold (and can infect humans too!)

- Parainfluenza - a viral infection of the upper respiratory system that causes the infamous kennel cough and can also cause pneumonia

- Parvovirus - in many geographies the most prevalent viral infection of all. It affects the lining of the intestinal tract which can cause severe vomiting and diarrhea, and hence weakens the immune system, thus often causing secondary infections that affect the entire body (often fatal!)

- Coronavirus - a viral infection similar to the Parvovirus, but with a different effect on the intestinal tract and typically *not* fatal.

Please note that what you can find on the internet about canine vaccinations is totally outdated - and much of it was never correct from the start (I know because I intensely searched for it myself, and I am shocked by what I found). On the internet, if just *one* publishes nonsense, it gets proliferated by the thousands within mere weeks: People love the ease of copying, not the effort of research.

So, if you are only mildly worried about getting the right vaccinations for your dog (and *only* those!), I strongly suggest that you study the comprehensive and most up-to-date Periodical on vaccinations on our site. You will be glad you did: mygermanshepherd.org/periodical/dog-vaccinations-and-puppy-vaccinations

Yes, of course it does apply to any dog breed or mix. In case you don't read that Periodical, a final note right here:

Never try to 'home-vaccinate' your puppy (or adult dog)! The risk of allergic reaction and blood disorder could make you literally watch your dog *die* within minutes (unlike with humans, there exist 8 major canine blood types, plus a few rare ones).

So, *always* have vaccinations done by a vet or animal clinic. Spend the few dollars to save yourself trouble and to save your pup's life and well-being. - Flea and Tick remedies are *not* vaccinations - those you may give to your puppy yourself. But very few you can safely give before age 3 months (for more see here:

mygermanshepherd.org/periodical/best-flea-treatment-for-dogs-and-best-flea-control-for-dogs)

When to Start Puppy Training

At what age, and at what time during the day is it appropriate to train our puppy, to *develop* our puppy?

Right Age to Start Puppy Training

Reputable Breeders (p~35) and Dog Shelters/ Breed Rescue Centers (p~37) will normally not give you a puppy that's younger than about 8 weeks (see Family Socialization, p~66).

Because, until this age the puppy needs its mother and fellow litter more than you. Also, there is a strict regiment of initial pack socialization and vaccinations that reputable breeders and dog rescue centers will follow. This is to ensure that when you get your pup it can be considered safe - for both of you.

There is no need to worry that an older puppy might not develop full bonding with you - it will, provided of course that you treat it well.

Even an abandoned dog of say 6 years of age at a **shelter or rescue centre** will develop full bonding with you if you treat the dog well.

Naturally, if the handler changes, this will first put stress on the dog. Nonetheless, every dog will fully bond with its new handler within a few weeks if treated well. This is a bit harder with a traumatized dog, but perfectly achievable as well.

And the right training does the rest - that's what the remainder of this book is about. The *right* puppy training. A dog training that helps us to build the best relationship with our puppy, and to maintain this throughout our dog's life.

So, the right age to start puppy training ideally is *before* any problems begin to develop. This means, when we get our pup at age 8 weeks or later, we *immediately* start with the puppy training principles as set out in the following chapters.

There is no 'too early' here. And thankfully, no 'too late' either.

Right Time for Puppy Training

Next, what is the right time of day to train our pup?

Let's find this out as well:

Ideally, puppies until about three or even four months of age should get four small meals, spread out over the entire day. This is for very different reasons:

- At a young age the intestinal tract cannot cope with a couple of large meals. Also, particularly the larger breed puppies grow so quickly during the first 7 months of their life that, if the same growth rate applied to humans, we would be about the size of a *bus* by the age of 5!
- Four small meals, spread out over the entire day, better cope with both these facts.
- In addition, the more meals we give our pup, the more chances we have for puppy training and relationship building (see in Feeding Routine, p~104).

For the same physiological reasons as set out above, it is paramount to encourage our puppy to DRINK A LOT during the day. How much our pup should drink each day primarily depends on its weight and exercise. But rather than adhering to some specific *amount* of water, better just make sure that there's always a bowl available filled with fresh water, day and night.

If you notice that your puppy doesn't feel tempted to drink much water, you can add the water of a can of (unsalted) tuna, or two ice cubes - for many dogs both are much loved additions (and the tuna is very healthy too).

It makes no sense when new puppy owners (sort of) 'convince themselves': "If I give my pup less to drink, it needn't pee that often and potty accidents are less likely".

Then they could likewise argue: "If I don't have a puppy at all, potty accidents become impossible - unless I get Diarrhea myself". Speaking of it, **Diarrhea** actually is a symptom of **Constipation** - which accounts for lifelong intoxication of our bloodstream from the garbage bag we carry around with us in our GI tract!

For dogs as well as for us, this permanent gastrointestinal intoxication is a prime reason for many illnesses (from arthritis to cancer), see the incredibly helpful book Cure Constipation Now from Dr Wes Jones: mygermanshepherd.org/go/book-cure-constipation-now.

With the right Potty Training (p~192) approach, accidents can be limited to a period of about one week only. Other than this, we cannot get both: A puppy, *and* no need to potty-walk it frequently.

No, regardless of breed, a pup until about age three months needs to get a potty chance every 60 minutes, and during night time when the metabolism is reduced, every 2 hours.

Because:

- The bladder of a puppy is so small and undeveloped that without frequent potty chances potty accidents are unavoidable.

- When dogs cannot relieve themselves frequently, urinary tract infections (mygermanshepherd.org /my-german-shepherd/german-shepherd-health /german-shepherd-bladder-infection) develop *much* quicker than in humans (that's why dogs in the wild often pee every 20 to 60 min!).

So, taking into account the frequent meal times and potty times as explained above, the right time for dedicated puppy training is already very limited: Obviously our pup cannot concentrate on training when it has just eaten, or it is very hungry, or it urgently needs to relieve itself, or when it feels sleepy.

However, getting *four* smaller meals spread out over the entire day avoids that our puppy gets very hungry - despite the incredible growth during puppy development.

This means, the ideal time for dedicated puppy training are <u>the two hours before each meal</u>

But we need to take two more considerations into account.

1. If we do it right, puppy training happens *all the time*, because initially every situation is new to our pup. And, showing a puppy how we would like it to behave in a new situation, well, that is training! That's why I spoke before about *dedicated* puppy training, which should be provided during the two hours before each meal.

2. The attention span of a young puppy is very limited. So, we cannot require from our pup dedicated training during the entire two hours before each meal. Indeed, for a puppy that is 8 weeks old, a dedicated training session that exceeds 30 to 60 *seconds* can be too long already. And until about 6 months of age a puppy should not receive training sessions of more than 10 min maximum, with breaks of at least 20 min in between.

Now, taking all the above points into account:

The right time for dedicated puppy training is between 4 and 6 times during the two hours before each meal

This gives us between 16 to 24 dedicated training sessions per day, and between 102 to 168 per week (a day-off is not needed for this type of training). This is plenty; certainly more than we need in order to raise the dog we want.

That is, if we have so much time ourselves! Most of us need to work, collect the kids, get some groceries etc, so we may not always be able to provide these dedicated training sessions anyway.

And, much more important than the *frequency* of puppy training is that we provide the *right* training approach to our pup - which is the purpose of this book.

Solving All the Common Puppy and Dog Behavior Problems!

Many of the common dog problems may be familiar to you from your own experience:

- Not coming when called
- Pulling on the lead
- Urinating and/or defecating all around the place
- Making your furniture look like a scratchcard
- Chewing on your shoes and other belongings
- Chasing you, or road participants, or animals
- Playing a game of 'Catch me if you can'
- Digging up the garden
- Barking the hell out of your night's sleep
- Whining as if it was the last day on earth
- Jumping up on you or strangers
- and... Nibbling or Biting you, or family members, friends, relatives, or strangers!

In our human interpretation, all these are *dog problems.*

All the common puppy and dog problems can be limited if not entirely solved by developing the right mindset and then applying our NO-Force, NO-Fear, NO-Fuss Puppy Training!

In fact, most puppy problems and dog problems disappear *quietly* when we apply our specific puppy training approach.

This will become apparent in the following chapters. Be prepared to be amazed! :-)

The PRIME SECRET about Dogs

The majority of the dog experts in the world agree now that the key to successful puppy and dog training is that we maintain a position as Pack leader for our dog.

And some dog experts, typically those who are rather limited to dog *training*, make us believe that everything that's not right with our dog is because we are not vigorously demonstrating our position as Pack leader.

Initially, and still while I researched and studied various subjects of canine sciences, I agreed with the view that our role as Pack leader is the key to 'raising the dog we want'.

However, a few years ago I suddenly realized that this is *not* the key. I had that 'light bulb' moment - although it felt more like a stadium's flood-lighting. A genuine Eureka moment.

What I am going to share with you in this chapter is so unique that no famous dog trainer anywhere in the world has published this yet.

Read the publications from say Cesar Millan, Joel Silverman, Don Sullivan, Dan Abdelnoor (Doggy Dan), John Garcia, Barbara Woodhouse, Ian Dunbar, Victoria Stilwell, Mia Montagliani, Patricia McConnell, Jean Donaldson, Pat Miller, Turid Rugaas, Alexandra Semyonova, Leslie McDevitt, Sophia Yin, Karen Pryor, Susan Garrett, Suzanne Clothier, Carol Lea Benjamin, Monks of New Skete, and any other well-known dog trainer that would have made this list too long.

Read them all. *None* of them has published this.

I call this **the PRIME SECRET about dogs**.

Because I observed that when we understand this 'Prime Secret' about dogs, it helps us more than anything else to 'raise the dog we want', to avoid all the common dog problems, and even to prevent certain health issues and premature death!

:

:

Suspense maxed?

Good!

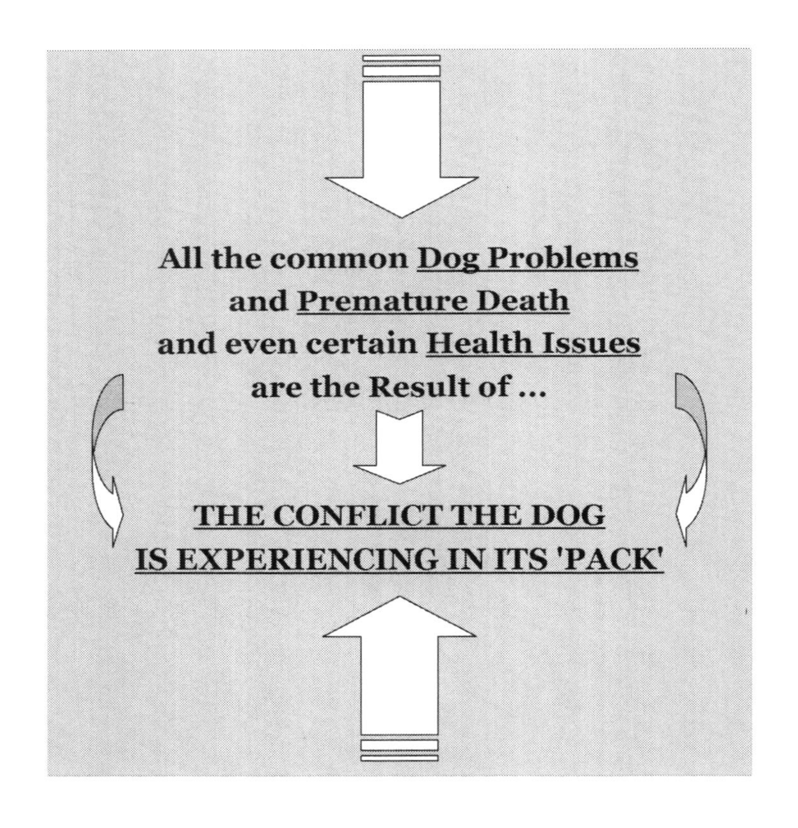
All the common Dog Problems
and Premature Death
and even certain Health Issues
are the Result of ...
THE CONFLICT THE DOG
IS EXPERIENCING IN ITS 'PACK'

Let me explain:

Dogs struggle with their perceived role as 'Pack' leader, and this struggle can be observed as early as age 8 or 9 weeks for most breeds - the time when most people are just getting their new puppy.

During **Family Socialization**, and very pronounced with **Puberty**, puppies start to become more and more autonomous and dominant (see Puppy Development Timeline, p~64). This burst is induced or exacerbated by the fact that the pup is now typically separated from its litter mates and mother, and it is now with a human family pack: us.

From the owner's behavior (that's you, me, or any other dog owner), the puppy now partly gets the impression that it is the Pack leader already: The pup *can do what it wants* to get our attention, and - if we've got a large breed puppy - it may soon even *drag us* on a leash behind.

However, the conflict arises because naturally any dog struggles with this role! Every day, maybe every hour. Because, in countless situations the dog has to experience that it is not the accepted Pack leader:

- The owner always commands the dog around, inside and outside of the house.
- The owner decides over the walk by opening the door or leaving it closed.

- The owner even puts a collar around the dog's neck, and keeps the dog on a leash - and pulls, tears, and drags the dog via the connection leash - collar - neck - throat!

- Worst of all, the owner determines when, what, and how much food the dog gets to eat!

All this, and much more, makes clear to the dog that it has to continue to prove its leader status in the Pack - like it would do in the wild - until it is the accepted Pack leader, or until it is outperformed by another Pack leader.

I am sure that very, very few dog owners, dog experts, and dog trainers recognize that indeed dogs notice this conflict, and how much **stress** this conflict puts on the dog.

Why?

Because the two most fundamental genetic canine quests are affected:

1. To secure food

2. To belong to a Pack, either as accepted Pack member or as accepted Pack leader - every unclear position means struggle, fight, until the positions are clear

Both is a genetically driven quest of every dog (unless traumatized). So, no way that the dog doesn't suffer a conflict!

The dog suffers a conflict for as long as it *thinks* it is the Pack leader but also experiences that this is contested by the dog owner (and all family pack members!) - every day again. Every hour. Maybe every minute of being together!

This conflict will only end when the owner's behavior clearly and consistently shows the dog that it is no longer the Pack leader. That the dog can now *relax*. Like in the wild, when a new, stronger dog takes over the leadership of the Pack.

Only at this point, all the other dogs submit to the new Alpha, the new Pack leader. And only until the Pack leader shows first signs of weakness - at which point the dogs will again fight over the positions in the Pack.

On the other hand, almost every dog happily accepts a submissive position in the Pack - as long as there is a clear Pack leader - that always leaves some food behind.

Note the 'as long as'.

Conclusion: The key to successful puppy training and dog training is not that we maintain a position as Pack leader for our dog. Instead, the key is that we know how to reduce or eliminate the conflict our dog is experiencing in its Pack - so that we become the *accepted* Pack leader.

The consequence of this discovery is that we all need to re-consider how we interact with our dogs and our puppies, so that we are and remain the *accepted* Pack leader throughout the day. Every day. Throughout our dog's entire life.

Note that *acceptance* as Pack leader does not even *permit* to employ force, or to raise fear, or to bribe with food treats!

Because all of that does not lead to acceptance, instead:

- force and fear lead to plain obedience
- and food treats lead to opportunism.

Only acceptance permits to develop a relationship that is based on love

Never forget this crucial point.

This further documents why it is essential that we focus on becoming the *accepted* Pack leader for our puppy. Which, in turn, requires that we reduce or eliminate the conflict that our dog is experiencing in its Pack! You see, it all makes sense. As it should.

This is quite something to chew on! For us, this time. ;-)

However, it is fascinating to observe just how much our dog-human relationship improves once we understand this conflict and we implement a few initial steps to reduce it! Wow!

So let's delve in right now, so that we can implement the most basic steps to reduce this conflict as early as:

TODAY!

How to Become the *Accepted* Pack Leader

Once we understand that the key is to become the accepted Pack leader, we can aim to reduce or eliminate this conflict that the dog is experiencing in its Pack.

For your puppy, you and every member in your family are part of your pup's Pack, of your pup's family.

Important is to understand that every human family member must be positioned as Pack leader to your puppy. For example, if you are not around but say your 5-year old is looking after the pup while you are getting some groceries from the corner shop, then your puppy must know that it is subordinate to your 5-year old as being the Pack leader!

If this hierarchy, with our dog being *last*, is not properly implemented then we get those dog problems (see the chapter 'Solving All the Common Puppy and Dog Behavior Problems', p~86) that we all know of, at least from the news: "Boy bitten by dog while mum was away", or "Docile puppy turned into aggressive beast", and the like.

So, how can we achieve that our puppy accepts every family member as Pack leader?

Is it sufficient if our children generously give food treats to our pup or indeed do all of the feeding?

No. Instead, we must systematically address each of the key areas that create the conflict that our pup is experiencing in its Pack.

Accordingly, in this book we will focus on:

- Puppy Attention Seeking
- Puppy Feeding Routine
- Puppy Leash Training

Puppy Attention Seeking

The younger the dog, the more we (and even strangers) feel that urge to give our full attention. Typically, a small puppy is so cute that we cannot resist to cuddle it when we merely see it, and we pamper our pup all day long.

And at night we don't stop either: We let it sleep in our bed(room), we nurse it at the slightest impression it might be hungry, and we literally push an array of toys to our pup, etc.

No matter how you put it, fact is though that our own behavior here creates a multitude of puppy problems right now, and massive dog problems later. The real problem for our dog however is that we later consider everything as dog problems - although all of them are the result of our own problem: earlier not knowing how to treat our puppy the right way.

Learning to pay no attention to our puppy unless we ask for our pup's attention, this is the hardest bit of the right puppy training, yet it is the crucial part of the right puppy training. Note that 'Learning to pay no attention' relates to ourselves: We must learn this, not our pup. Indeed, puppy training - like all dog training - is very much a two-way road.

Hardest for us, nonetheless best for our puppy is that we learn to **ignore** our pup. Not in a cruel way, but in the *right way*.

Why is a certain degree of *ignoring* **best** for a puppy?

In short:

- This shows our dog that it may *relax*, it doesn't constantly have to try to *please* us (a trait that has been bred into canines for up to 33,000 years!)

- This substantially **reduces** the *conflict* our dog is experiencing in its family pack (see The Prime Secret about Dogs, p~88)

- *And* it is exactly the feedback our puppy would get in its animal pack too (and indeed *did* get during Litter Socialization, p~65)

We must never forget that even the cutest puppy on the planet after all is not a child but an *animal* - that deserves that its genetic *canine traits* are being appreciated.

Therefore, crucially, we should ignore excessive attention-seeking - unless of course our puppy might be ill or in pain, is thirsty or hungry, or needs a potty walk.

How to Ignore the *Right* Way

Ideally, we merely turn away or walk away. Where not possible, we *gently* move away our pup (ideally with the *outside* of our arm, else with the back of our hand), in a *calm* movement. Important: We do not look at our pup now, nor do we speak to our pup, nor do we touch our pup at this time.

Why?

Because, already a young dog of age 8 weeks notices our body language, tone of voice, energy level, mood etc much better than we will ever notice our dog's. Thus, for any form of behavior correction we should act as *apathetic* as we can, to not (unconsciously) *confuse* our pup with aspects of our *mood.*

Example: We are sitting on the couch and not even doing anything. Just sitting there. This is of course a perfect situation for our puppy to come over and cuddle our legs, or jump on our lap or lay its head on our lap. Particularly, when we open our legs even just a tiny bit, it looks to our pup like an invitation to collect a cuddle from us.

But we really should not show any sign of affection *at this moment.* Because we did not actually invite our puppy to collect a cuddle. Thus we will now use the *outside* of our arm (ideally; otherwise the outside of our hand) to *gently* move our pup away. We won't say anything, we won't touch our pup, and we won't look down at it.

Now, of course puppies have it that we can't easily move them away without them coming back immediately. Yes, our puppy will be persistent in trying to collect a cuddle or get on our lap. And we will show the same persistence in using the *outside* of our arm to *gently* move our pup away.

After three or four times either our puppy will have understood, or we usually will experience some discomfort moving our pup away, right?

Now we *have* to get up from our couch and walk away! We may need to go into another room of the house - still, our puppy may follow us. So, we may need to go in yet another room and close the door behind us.

Now comes the critical part: Our puppy may whine or bark or scratch at the door like it was the last day on earth! (Door scratchguards can help in such case: mygermanshepherd.org/go/door-scratchguard)

Yet, we must try to do whatever we wanted to do in that room. This may feel very hard right now, but the payoff for the rest of our dog's life (and for our own life) is totally worth it, because once our puppy learned that we do not give attention unless we want to, we and our puppy will relax in all such future situations!

Conversely, if we now give in then:

- Our puppy will have learned nothing from it
- Our puppy will get a confirmation that it is the leader of the pack who determines attention
- This perceived confirmation will *increase* the conflict our puppy is experiencing (because in many other moments our behavior still makes clear that our pup is *not* the pack leader), and
- This conflict that our puppy is experiencing will continue to create massive **stress** for our pup (as well as for us!)

Indeed, when you have a puppy that is following you everywhere, wagging its tail like it has to clean the floor, staring up at you, maybe whining and barking at you... - then what you really have is: a very stressed young dog!

Naturally, such regular (or almost permanent!) stress is not good for our dog at all, and much less for a young puppy. It is exactly these dogs that I just described, that accumulate many health problems during their short life and then often experience premature death - plus, high vet bills for their owners.

I would love to see a systematic study of the relationship between the number of dogs that behave the way just described, and their medical records and lifespans, and a comparison group of dogs that received a puppy training and dog training that, yes, allowed them to relax (and us too).

Unfortunately, no such studies have yet been undertaken (neither breed-specific nor across various dog breeds), because our NO-Force, NO-Fear, NO-Fuss Puppy Training approach is still too new. Dogs trained this way haven't yet died.

But, based on all my observations (and plain common sense really!), I am convinced that such studies would outright confirm that dogs that received the *right* training (in order for them to *relax*, and for us to *relax* too) live considerably longer and healthier lives. - Other things being equal!

More so, dogs that received the *right* training don't create all the dog problems (p~86) - which really are nothing other than our human interpretation of canine behavior that doesn't meet our expectations.

Puppy Feeding Routine

Ideally, give your puppy *four* meals a day, at fixed meal times, until about age 3 or 4 months, and then reduce this to *three* daily meals until at least age 7 or 8 months.

Under Right Time for Puppy Training (p~81) I mentioned that the more meals we give our pup, the more chances we have for puppy training and relationship building, and I said I would later explain this a bit more. This is now.

Each time before we serve our puppy a meal (not a simple food treat), we make a performance of **Gesture Eating** in front of our pup's eyes:

- We symbolically - or literally, if we like the taste :-) - eat a bit of our pup's meal from its bowl, so to say spooning it into our mouth (pretending it)

- With a puppy younger than 3 months we should really 'make a point' and do this for at least a minute

- Then we ask our pup to SIT a bit further back (usually puppies will move back anyway when they see this!)

- Only then we place down the bowl for our pup

- Still, we don't want our pup to eat the meal immediately, because that would encourage scavenging (mygermanshepherd.org/periodical/how-to-stop-scavenging) any food outside that it may find. We want our pup to wait for our signal to go to its bowl and eat

- Only then our pup eats - and we will normally not disturb our puppy during its meal!

Note that we only put down our pup's bowl when (s)he is sitting calm, not as long as (s)he is standing, wagging its tail, whining or barking.

What to Do if Our Pup is Not Calm During Gesture Eating?

We simply postpone the meal. We put it back and do whatever we want to do. Then, after 5, 10, or 15 minutes, we come back and make another attempt. Do no more than 3 attempts though!

If our puppy is still not calm during our Gesture Eating, we cancel the meal.

This is no problem at all, because our pup is on 4 meals a day! It won't starve, not even feel really hungry, if it doesn't get this meal.

But what this will do is, it will demonstrate to our pup that we are the Pack leader, who eats first, like in the wild. The added beauty of this procedure is: It will demonstrate our Pack leadership whether or not we had to cancel the meal!

What if Our Pup Later is on 3 Meals a Day?

First, when we have done this Gesture Eating consistently for some time, then by the age of 3 or 4 months our puppy will long ago have learned to be calm during meal times. So, there will hardly be a need to cancel any meal.

Second, even if we need to cancel one of three meals a day, this is no problem at all, our pup won't starve when it gets just two meals a day. In fact, we know that wild dogs' puppies that are 3 months old survive three or more *days* without any food - but not even a single day without water!

So, getting no meal for the next 8 hours or so certainly does no harm at all (heck, some puppy owners never even feed more than *one* meal a day). Conversely, during the next meal time, watch and see: Your pup will behave very different already.

And What if Our Pup is Not Calm During Several Consecutive Meal Times?

I would suggest to cancel up to three consecutive meals if on 3 or 4 meals a day (so, possibly, one day without food).

And in such case, instead of the fourth attempt I would then put down the bowl with the meal some-where else (to prevent the *conditioning* of undesirable behavior), and simply open that door so that our pup can find the food through smell.

Note: I wouldn't at all encourage our pup to look for the food, nor would I point in the direction or anything like that. I would **just apathetically open the door** to where I have put down the bowl with the meal.

Do not worry about too little food intake. But do worry about too little water intake - always provide plenty!

Needless to say, but good to consider: Being calm during meal times significantly impacts how quickly our puppy - and later our adult dog - is eating.

Dogs that we see gulping down their food as if it was the last meal in their life (dogs don't really know if it isn't) are stressed dogs.

Both, gulping down the food and **stress** do increase the likelihood of a multitude of health issues, like

Bloat or Gastric Torsion (mygermanshepherd.org/ my-german-shepherd/german-shepherd-health/ger man-shepherd-bloat-or-gastric-torsion - the latter being a particular risk for the larger breeds), Gastro-enteritis or Pancreatitis (mygermanshepherd.org/ my-german-shepherd/german-shepherd-health), Kidney Failure or Heart Failure (mygermanshepherd .org/my-german-shepherd/german-shepherd-health).

Not to forget the more obvious and more immediate consequences like Vomiting (mygermanshep-herd.org /my-german-shepherd/german-shepherd-health/ger man-shepherd-vomiting) and/or Diar-rhea (mygerma nshepherd.org/my-german-shepherd/german-sheph erd-health/german-shepherd-diarrhea).

Now, really crucial is further: If ever our puppy goes away from any food (ie including food treats), we immediately take the food away and cancel the meal or food treat!

If we were to leave the food in the bowl or on the ground, so that our pup can come back later and eat at its own will, then:

- We would make our pup think that it has control over food (being the most fundamental genetic canine quest, see The Prime Secret about Dogs, p~88), and

- Again, we would increase the conflict that our puppy is experiencing in its pack, instead of **reducing** it

- We would encourage scavenging (mygerman-shepherd.org/periodical/how-to-stop-scavenging) any 'food' items that our dog may find on the ground.

As dog lovers, we want none of this, because it wouldn't be in our pup's best interest.

Combining the Feeding Routine with Bite Inhibition Training

As mentioned above, we will normally *not* disturb our puppy during its meal. However, there is an exception, namely where a brief disturbance of the meal has more advantages than disadavantages. This exception is **Bite Inhibition Training**.

Key parts of Bite Inhibition Training belong to the **Feeding Routine**:

- Briefly taking away the food bowl
- Briefly interrupting meals to add a tasty morsel
- Hand-feeding morsels

We should do this regularly (once a day is okay, so a good rule of thumb is with every third meal and food treat). This trains our pup not to nip (p~243) or bite (p~249) us even when we intervene in the pup's prime concern: securing food!

Note: For safety reasons, initially only you may do any of this, not your children - until you see from your kids' Gesture Eating (p~104) that your puppy remains calm all the time.

Also, upon the first growl or snarl (or rigid tail or other body language signal), immediately stop and postpone, or *calm down* your pup first - using our

Sedatives from the Dog Training Toolkit (mygermanshepherd.org/go/dog-training-toolkit) will help.

Bite Inhibition got its own chapter later in the book, see Bite Inhibition Training (p~162).

Puppy Leash Training

The third key area that creates the conflict that our pup is experiencing in its Pack is **Leash Training** (for the urban and suburban dogs that get leash walks). Again, here we will only address the points that are relevant for the purpose of this chapter: How to Become the *Accepted* Pack Leader (p~96).

Nonetheless, we will not restrict this to a short leash training exercise. No, brace yourself for some long leash training. (I couldn't resist the pun! :-)

Before we can consider Leash Training, of course we need the right collar for our puppy:

Puppy Collars

With a small puppy, we leave the collar on all the time. Obviously this is for safety reasons, but also for training purposes:

There will come many situations where we need to be able to walk to our pup and restrain it by the collar. Be it to perform the Collar Freeze (p~142) or lead it into Isolation (p~145), or to take our pup on a short lead to do some SSCD (p~116), or to hold it back from some scavenging (mygermanshepherd. org/periodical/how-to-stop-scavenging) or chewing (p~212) temptation, etc.

While inside and at night time, we use a *soft* leather collar without those popular studs, certainly without spikes (safety concerns). While outside, a reflective collar like the one from Rogz (mygermanshepherd. org/go/rogz-reflective-dog-collar) or at least a red leather collar (mygermanshepherd.org/go/soft-leath er-collar) is safer, unless our puppy is strong and large, in which case we may want to get a wide, heavy-duty leather collar (mygermanshepherd.org/ go/heavy-duty-leather-collar) for our pup.

Why ideally leather collar?

Because a natural leather collar does provide a feel-good factor that synthetic collars (and certainly metal/chain collars) cannot provide. If you don't believe this, get both types and try them for one day each (on yourself ;-)

You too will observe that your pup will make nothing of having the leather collar around its neck, while it may intensely try to get off any other collar (particularly metal/chain ones of course).

If you have a strong and large puppy, you can alternatively consider to use a quality harness (mygerman shepherd.org/go/dog-harness) while outside. The reason would be that you don't want to make your pup feel strangled at its neck(!) in case the dog is pulling strongly (in which case you have a leash training problem). In such case a harness is much more gentle on your pup.

But again, when back inside, better put on a light *soft* padded leather collar - and leave this on all the time.

Now on to Leash Training!

SSCD

SSCD (Start - Stop - Change Direction) works like this:

- Attach a short lead to your puppy's collar
- Start to walk slowly in one direction
- Stop when *you* want to, or when your puppy pulls (in any direction!)
- Change Direction

Repeat this SSCD for a few minutes, or until your pup is totally calm: Always, start to walk slowly in one direction, then stop whenever you want to or when your puppy pulls (in any direction), and then turn to change direction.

We can do **SSCD** both indoors and outdoors, and it can serve four purposes:

1. Leash Training
2. Behavior Modification
3. Sedative
4. Distraction Tool

For the latter two I have to refer to the Dog Training Toolkit (mygermanshepherd.org/go/dog-trainin g-toolkit).

SSCD is significantly relaxing for a dog - unless the dog *hates* the leash. To prevent that, follow the subsequent advice how to introduce the leash the *right* way.

We don't actually start leash training our puppy using SSCD, we start leash training as I describe it in the following chapter: Short Leash Training. The reason why I presented SSCD beforehand is to give it its own chapter for easy navigation.

Short Leash Training

When we get our puppy (typically at age 8 weeks or older; see the chapter 'Right Age to Start Puppy Training', p~79), on the second day of having our pup, we immediately start with leash training, and we follow the steps below:

Stage 1

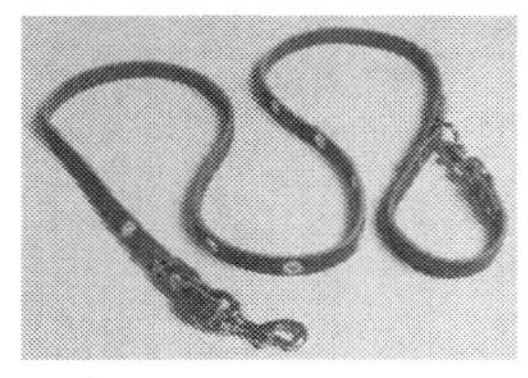

On the second day we have our pup, we attach a suitable short lead to the collar, at least three times a day, each for around 20 minutes or so.

Tip: You can straight away get the ultimate short lead, the leather training lead (mygermanshepherd. org/go/teaching-lead) from Sarah Hodgson, because there is no point in spending money twice on the same type of lead. Exception: For a small dog or toy breed this leash is too heavy.

Now, we let our puppy run around inside the house with the lead attached to its collar. This way our pup will get used to something hanging off its neck, and will not make a fuzz out of it later, each time we put on the lead.

Tip: So that your pup doesn't get tangled up around some furniture in the house, *don't* clip the second carabiner into the D-ring at the end of the lead (if it has one at all, like Sarah Hodgson's training lead has); just let the end hang loosely.

Every now and then, we gently step our foot on the end of the lead to make our pup stop in its track. Our puppy will then look up at us and wonder: "What's happening now, why does my Pack buddy hold me back?" (Remember, we are not yet the *accepted* Pack *leader*.)

In every such moment, we MUST give our pup a positive experience: Either we pat or, we say something like "good dog" or, if you really want to, give a tiny food treat and pat and say "good dog" (*we* don't give food treats for training).

Important: IF you give a food treat, combine it with praise *and* with patting your puppy - or you would devalue the non-food treats from your puppy's viewpoint. Remember: You don't want your dog to *expect* to get food treats, or do you?

On the second day of this **puppy lead training** (ie the third day we have our dog), every now and then - instead of just stepping on the end of the lead - we step on it to pick up the lead, reward our pup for stopping as described above, and then to initiate the first experience of *gentle* SSCD (p~116).

Repeat SSCD for a few minutes. Just don't overdo it, there's no point in getting your new puppy follow all your movements just yet, this is entirely about FUN from your pup's viewpoint.

Keep on practicing this **first part of leash training** over the first three days *inside* the house. Don't let your puppy outside yet, unless you have an enclosed garden and your pup already got all *relevant* vaccines (p~72). Safety first!

This is how to start puppy leash training the *right way*, how to start **successful puppy leash training**.

Long Leash Training

Stage 2

Given our pup already got all *relevant* vaccines (p~72), on the fourth day of lead training (day 5 of having our new pup), the outdoor leash training starts, with a long leash:

We attach a suitable long lead or long line to the collar and go with our puppy out into the garden or another safe area close-by, again at least three times a day, each for around 20 minutes or so.

Tip: You can straight away get the ultimate long line, the very light 50 feet long outdoor line (mygermansh epherd.org/go/long-line) from Sarah Hodgson: As said before, there is no point in spending money twice on the same type of lead.

With the long line attached, we let our pup run around freely within that safe space.

At this stage, the purpose is *not* to restrain our puppy in any way, at any time. We don't step on the long line - unless there's danger of course, that's the whole point of the long line: that our dog can run freely but we retain ultimate control.

Instead, the purpose of this phase of **puppy lead training** is that our pup simply gets used to running around freely, and outside, while something is hanging off its neck.

During these next couple of days, we give our new puppy as much opportunity as we have time to let it explore the (limited) surroundings within that safe space.

This is the **second stage of successful puppy leash training**.

Note that the beginning of the outdoor leash training already considers the **purpose of the lead**:

The *only* purpose of the lead or leash is that we have a physical restraint when the trained restraint (the Recall, p~127) cannot yet be expected to work for sure in the given situation.

Since we haven't yet trained our puppy the Recall, we MUST have at least a long line attached when we go outside the house (again, safety first).

Stage 3

At the third stage of puppy lead training (about day 6), we start the **leash training** as part of **dog walking**:

We plan a session of an hour or so, and we take *both* leads with us, the *short lead* and the *long lead*.

Once we are in our chosen safe space, we attach the short lead to our pup's collar, and now *briefly* do some 'real' SSCD (p~116) in that open space (no more than 2 minutes each).

Real SSCD means that now the focus is no longer entirely on FUN for our pup (although it should still have FUN, that's why we do very short sessions), instead the focus now is on **matching our movements** - and in a much more distractive environment for a young puppy!

Again, don't overdo it, but do get your puppy to **start** when you start walking, to **stop** when you stop walking, and to **change direction** when you change direction - and in the same direction. :-)

After each two minutes (with lots of affection and/or praise for matching our movements!), swap the short leash for the long leash and let your pup freely 'roam' within that safe space for 10 minutes or so.

The purpose of these breaks is for our puppy to *relax* - to continue to experience this third lead training stage as FUN.

On each subsequent day, we choose **new environments** (subject to being safe), because the whole point of leash training as a physical substitute for the Recall is that the **Recall** shall later work *regardless* of the environment, regardless of the distractions in new situations!

Dogs do not easily transfer trained behavior in one situation and environment to the required behavior in another situation and environment

Conclusion for our unique approach to Puppy Leash Training (p~113):

Follow these three stages of successful Puppy Leash Training, and you will notice that each stage gently leads to the ultimate goal of Leash Training: Training the Recall.

This recommended approach to Puppy Leash Training normally means that within just one week our new puppy is lead-experienced and lead-conform in all standard situations.

On all days after this first week, we will simply **extend the experience for our pup**: We will conduct the Lead Training in varying environments and situations.

Reminder: The leash must never be tense - when it's tense, we stop! When our puppy pulls (in any direction), we stop! - We do some SSCD until our pup is calm again. If our pup is not calm, we go nowhere!

This may sometimes require that we freeze for a few minutes. But these breaks are well spent: Our puppy will learn *the gentle way* how we expect it to behave on leash.

Conclusion for How to Become the *Accepted* Pack Leader (p~96):

We must systematically address each of the key areas that create the conflict that our pup is experiencing in its Pack: Puppy Attention Seeking (p~98), Puppy Feeding Routine (p~104), and Puppy Leash Training (p~113).

There are of course more areas that contribute to the said conflict, but the above are the most important areas, which is why I wanted to include them for you in this book.

When we address these key areas in the way described above, we successfully *reduce* the conflict that our pup is experiencing: We demonstrate to our puppy that we are always the Pack leader.

Now our puppy does no longer get conflicting feedback from us - at least not in these three key areas of a dog's life!

When we follow this approach, we will notice that - already by the end of the same day that we start - our puppy is becoming a different dog: Much calmer, more relaxed, and more willing to wait for our signals.

Important is that we continue to follow this approach, because - in general - the acceptance as Pack leader must be earned every day anew, since striving for Pack leadership is the second-most fundamental genetic canine quest! See The Prime Secret about Dogs (p~88).

However, this will be *easy* for us when we make all of this NO-Force, NO-Fear, NO-Fuss Puppy Training our **routine**. We *routinely* apply all the points discussed in this book.

The Recall

The Recall is the real deal. It is the ultimate goal of leash training, and the proud of every dog owner.

Strangely then, for the owners of adult dogs and puppies alike, the **Recall** remains a very challenging training objective. And that's mainly because they don't know the key points about the Recall.

So, to make this chapter short, let's make a list of the key points for a successful Recall:

- Start with Leash Training (p107) immediately the day after you get your puppy. Don't let weeks or months pass by training to *call* your pup and giving affection just because 'it is so cute!'

- Hone all leash training stages as described, since leash training is at the heart of the Recall

- Train yourself to *ignore* your puppy whenever it comes *to you* without being called - This may appear 'harsh' to you but it is exactly how dogs learn to behave in their dog pack

- Be clear about what you want from your dog, be decisive, and don't confuse your dog with inconsistency

- Before each meal, always perform Gesture Eating

- Only ever give your puppy a meal, treats, praise, pats, cuddles and other affection when you have called your dog to you

- When you call your dog to you, and your dog doesn't immediately shoot towards you but then comes a bit later, ignore your dog - like (s)he just *decided* to ignore you to demonstrate his/her dominance in the Pack structure, as considered by your dog

In other words: Give your puppy only one chance to come when called - and then to get the reward you intended to give (which should always be something very worthwhile).

- If your pup decides not to make use of that one chance, then within a few times/days only (s)he will have completely understood that the chance is lost with the first call. Because thereafter your dog is being ignored - like the dog would be in its animal pack too

- Don't say anything when your pup just didn't come when called (like 'No, you just ignored me, now I ignore you', or 'This is part of your training, you see, you better come when I call you',...) - No, don't even look at your pup, no matter how begging or cute it looks

- Never call your dog away from its food or potty time, or indeed from anything which you can't beat (in terms of how great it is compared to what you have to offer)

- Find out what your puppy LOVES. Initially, motivate your pup to come immediately when called by *randomly* giving just that. Not every time (then it would lose its high attraction), but sometimes

- *Don't* focus on food treats, and randomize all rewards given

- Never use punishment (like threatening your dog with a harsh voice, actions, or longer-lasting withdrawal of attention and affection, food, potty-going, or similar)

Only when we have mastered all of the above, including all stages of Leash Training (p~113), we start to practice the Recall. This is done *outdoors*:

- First, go to a place where you are alone with your puppy, and after 5 minutes of SSCD with the short leash, switch to the long line (mygerma nshepherd.org/go/long-line)

- Say 'GO' (or whatever dog command (mygerma nshepherd.org/training-a-german-shepherd/dog -commands) you use to release your puppy in order to be free to do what it wants), and let your pup run around on its own account. Ensure that the long line always remains loose (ie in this case, go after your pup if needed)

- Then after a few minutes, call your puppy once (but make sure it heard you) and while doing so even *walk away*, indicating you are 'leaving'

- With all the inhouse training before (see above), your pup should now immediately speed to- wards you, *without* you showing a treat

- Indeed, never reveal the treat you have on offer - like arms wide open indicating affection, or a toy in hand, or a movement indicating play, or excited voice indicating praise, or waving a food treat, or whatever. Instead, always *surprise* your puppy.

If your pup doesn't shoot towards you, no problem, don't show any grudge. You have just tried your *first* Recall, practice the same routine more often now.

Crucial (often forgotten): Once the **Recall** is always successful in a place where you are alone with your puppy, practice the Recall under increasingly more distractive conditions: People nearby, other dogs nearby, a lonely large piece of meat at a barbecue, or any other highly attractive distraction.

Just remember not to overdo it: The *less* you call your dog (the less restrictive and/or dominant you are, really) the more impact it will have *when* you do it.

When you adopt the above key points, the relationship with your dog will be lifted onto another level of bonding and companionship!

Soon you too will notice the vast difference a **proper Recall** makes to the quality of life - for your dog as well as for yourself.

Reward Types

There are 5 Reward Types:

1. Praise
2. Affection (pats, cuddles, belly stroking, etc)
3. Toys and Play
4. Real-life rewards
5. Food treats

When can we use which?

- We use **Praise** only when we can control our energy state and tone of voice
- We use **Affection** when we cannot control our energy state and tone of voice, or to *lower* our dog's energy state, ie to make our puppy calmer
- We use **Toys and Play** when we want to *raise* our dog's energy state, ie to be more active
- With young puppies until about 3 to 4 months of age, we focus on Affection, Praise, and Toys & Play as a reward for behavior we desire

- With older puppies and adult dogs, we focus on **Real-Life Rewards** - which is an action our dog desires, for example:

  - Sniffing the ground for as long as our dog wants (because sniffing the ground is another fundamental genetic canine trait that we should never try to suppress; see the introduction to these in the chapter The Prime Secret about Dogs, p~88).

  - Extended outdoor exercise of whatever our puppy loves (swim, catch, fetch, jump, whatever)

  - Getting through the front door first, for an immediate walk

  - Running *off-leash* (in safe areas) - which by the way is *crucial* for every dog, for health and behavior reasons!

  - Providing a comfy place *near* us (in addition to the crate which should remain fixed at one place)

  - Anything our dog LOVES to do!

- Finally, we give **Food Treats** (being the fifth reward type) only when convenient for us and appropriate for our dog: Food Treats should not be the standard reward (for both health and behavior reasons), and Food Treats should always be more attractive than meals

- Whenever we give Food Treats, we deduct this *amount* from the upcoming meal, since we neither want an obese dog nor 'badger' it with molecular nibbles (like some modern 'dog trainers' in youtube videos are practicing) - however, for really small puppies peanut-sized nibbles are not 'badgering'.

Note: Even something as inconspicuous as **giving attention** can be a reward to our puppy - because *what our dog feels* determines whether it's a reward or not.

For example, a long look in our dog's eyes and smiling can mean a reward to our pup. So you could argue that **Attention** is a sixth reward type.

However, giving attention typically happens *subconsciously* for us, while employing one of the five reward types above is a much more conscious matter. Since we only reward our puppy for behavior we desire (see next, in The NO-Force, NO-Fear, NO-Fuss Puppy Training), it would appear wrong to count **Attention** as a form of reward.

The NO-Force, NO-Fear, NO-Fuss Puppy Training

With so much new content for you to absorb in the past chapters, I guess you may appreciate if I provide a sort of bullet-point summary of The NO-Force, NO-Fear, NO-Fuss Puppy Training, instead of many long paragraphs, right?

Okay, again let me try to sum up the key points of our unique Puppy Training approach:

- We never use force with our dog: We don't ever hit our pup, we don't push or pull, we don't kick, we don't use electronic collars and the like, we don't use *any form* of force at all!

- We never cause fear in our dog: We don't scare or frighten our pup, we don't threaten or caution it, we don't position us as despot manic with 'Obedience Training' - we don't want a cringing dog

- We never fuss around with our dog: We don't scream or shout, we don't use loud noises or rapid movements, we don't buy dog training gimmicks (mygermanshepherd.org/go/electronic-dog-training), and we don't make dog training the most important topic (it isn't - **Relationship Building** is more important)

- We never call our puppy to us or pull it to us (say, by using the lead) and then give it a *negative* experience (say, putting on the lead, scolding, or whatever) or no sign of a good reason

- Whenever we call our puppy to us, we *must* have a good reason - good reason meaning a positive experience for our dog (any of the 5 Reward Types, p~132)

- Whenever we want to do something that our puppy may not like - say, putting on the lead, performing dental hygiene (mygermanshepherd. org/periodical/gsd-mouth-care) or paw care (my germanshepherd.org/periodical/gsd-paw-care) - we must walk to our dog

When our puppy is 'naughty', we respond in one of only three ways:

- If we feel it's still 'okay' for a canine(!), we ignore it and forget about it (to some degree we should accept that dogs have different genes and a different understanding than children/humans)

- If it's lighter misconduct, we perform the Collar Freeze (see next chapter, p~142)

- If it's serious misconduct or *persistent* lighter misconduct, we immediately isolate (p~145) our puppy (again, see next chapter)

We like to **reward** our puppy, but not just for looking cute, or coming to us seeking our attention, or to collect a cuddle, patting, praise, or food treats:

- We only reward our puppy for behavior we desire

- We always give rewards that are appropriate to the behavioral achievement (rewards must be earned in a dog pack, and so should be in a family pack too)

- We randomize the reward types and the specific rewards we give, so that our dog does not learn to *expect* a certain reward from us.

The above is not a complete list of the key points of The NO-Force, NO-Fear, NO-Fuss Puppy Training, but it is a good list for now. It should allow you to take a BIG step (many steps) forward with your puppy training, and in your human-dog relationship.

The ONLY 'Punishment' You'll Ever Need

Look at the BIG names in the dog training industry, and you'll find that most of the famous dog trainers use one or more of the following in their dog training approach:

- force
- fear
- food treats (lots of/systematic)
- raised voice (shouting)
- electronic devices
- physical restraints

And/or they make simple things complex and package their dog training like an academic profession, giving it a different name (dog psychologist, dog behavior analyst, dog whisperer, dog listener, etc) to sell their courses at higher prices.

Many make much fuss about it, as we say.

The noteworthy exception among the famous dog trainers is Doggy Dan (Dan Abdelnoor) whose dog training approach is similar to ours. He has a fantastic online video training site (mygermanshepherd. org/go/online-dog-trainer) which is why we wholeheartedly recommend him if you need a *real* dog trainer, without spending a fortune on a dog trainer nearest to you - to get uncertain results yielded with unknown methods.

By the way, dog training is *not* an academic profession, nor is dog psychology or dog behavior analysis, not even 'whispering' or 'listening' to dogs.

Conversely, a profound and really interesting academic ' canine congress' is this regular meetup (csf2012.com), the largest of its kind.

Being dog lovers (see the book title), of course *force* as a training means we cannot tolerate at all.

And raising *fear* to get the desired behavior is the means of a despot, not of a loving dog parent (and is particularly bad for a puppy).

Both these means are punishment - instead of the much more successful motivation. Other authors (and most dog trainers) use the terms 'negative reinforcement' and 'positive reinforcement' - they sound so incredibly intellectual, don't they?

Well, frankly: they are nonsense. Explanation here. I now use the much clearer terms 'punishment' and 'motivation' - as that is what it's really about, right?

With force and fear being punishment, both these means have **undesirable side effects** - most notably both cause dog aggression!

And systematically using food treats is nothing but bribe - because dogs *do* have a memory. Particularly for anything relating to FOOD. Remember that securing food is the most fundamental genetic canine quest, see The Prime Secret about Dogs (p82). Thus, in general, dogs will do tomorrow whatever it takes to get extra FOOD like they got yesterday.

But this doesn't mean you've built a relationship with your dog, you've bribed - and once there is a better bribe (another dog, lost kebab or sausage on the road, whatever), your dog will go for that!

Indeed, when we consciously observe dog behavior, we can even see how dogs try one behavior after the other until they find the one that brings them the extra FOOD again. After all, exactly this trial & error approach is what is called *training*.

So, really, dogs *do* have a memory. Of course, some breeds better than others, and some dogs better than others of the same breed; see eg this great article (bit.ly/18EpJFz) from a funny-written dog science website (dogspies.com/Dog_Spies/Science!.html).

Back to our topic here: Our NO-Force, NO-Fear, NO-Fuss Puppy Training doesn't need any of these means (force, fear, food treats). Nor does it need shouting, electronic devices, or physical restraints.

No! No fuss at all!

Instead, we intensely focus on motivating our dog through our own behavior (p~19), and we use Rewards (p~132) as described in the prior chapter (so *not* with the focus on food treats). Any 'punishment' (for wrong-doing in the human view) is limited to the following two means, which are of course no punishment at all - since we are **dog lovers**:

- Collar Freeze
- Isolation

Both are explained subsequently.

If you want you could here also count in SSCD (p~116), since it too *can* serve the purpose of behavior modification. However:

a) I have already described SSCD under Leash Training (where it belongs), and

b) **Collar Freeze** and **Isolation** are *only* used for behavior modification - and the only two means really needed.

Collar Freeze

The Collar Freeze we use for lighter misconduct - say, chewing our shoes for the first time, or scavenging (mygermanshepherd.org/periodical/how -to-stop-scavenging) an item outside, or barking for too long (mygermanshepherd.org/periodical/end-gsd-excessive-barking) - from the canine viewpoint there is always a good reason for barking, but *we* may not like it.

The Collar Freeze will be a fascinating experience for you - until you get used to it, at which point you may wonder: "Why haven't I always been doing this?" :-)

Fascinating, because it appears so unlikely that this will do anything good - but it does! It makes everything good. That's what will fascinate you. It does with everyone. I am still fascinated about this myself.

What is the Collar Freeze?

Upon lighter misconduct of our puppy (misconduct in our view), we calmly walk to our pup and we *gently* take hold of our puppy's collar with one hand on the *underside*, not at the neck!

(Note: The bullet point list in the prior chapter, The NO-Force, NO-Fear, NO-Fuss Puppy Training (p~135), explained why we must walk to our pup; and with reference to the chapter Puppy Collars (p~114) it's now clear why the collar has to stay on all the time.)

We simply <u>hold</u> the collar, nothing else

Now <u>we</u> 'freeze': We stand still, we don't speak to our puppy, we don't touch our pup, and we don't look at it either. We appreciate that we are alive, that we have a pup, and that we got this book. We transmit our low energy to our puppy.

In fact, initially our puppy will *look at us* (all dogs do in this situation), but after a while it will no longer look up at us, and that's the first indication that our puppy is finally:

- calming down
- understanding that its behavior wasn't what we wanted
- and somehow 'saving a marker' in memory that seems to prevent repetition (immediately or soon).

Some puppies require the **Collar Freeze** several times for the same misconduct before 'it sinks in', other pups 'get the message' with the first Collar Freeze. The speed of learning doesn't only depend on the breed and specific dog, it also depends on *how you do it*: The more apathetic, the better (note what I highlighted in red above - probably more like greyish in the print edition, as two-color printing would have been even more expensive).

We 'freeze' until we feel that our pup is entirely calm and relaxed. This may take half a minute or five minutes, but it's time well spent: It not only calms our puppy, it is incredibly relaxing for ourselves too!

You deserve these breaks. Take them.

Isolation

Isolation we use for serious misconduct - any form of biting or uninvited nipping - this would be considered serious by mum and litter mates too! - or persistent lighter misconduct (say, chewing our shoes repetitively).

Uninvited nipping? Nipping outside dedicated Play/ Play-fighting (p~165).

Isolation may be a rather difficult experience for you - at least for the first couple of times, particularly if you have been one of the 'reward for cute looking' puppy parents. ;-)

What is Isolation?

Upon serious misconduct or persistent lighter misconduct, we immediately but calmly walk to our pup and lead it on the *underside* of the collar into Isolation: a small safe room, like for example a small tiled bathroom or any other room with as little distractions and furniture as possible.

A tiled small bathroom/ toilet room with an indoor potty (mygermanshepherd.org/go/ugodog) is ideal for this, even if we haven't done potty training with our puppy yet: We must not be upset if our pup is going to urinate while in Isolation (we just clean it up), but there is a chance that our pup may urinate on the indoor potty (and once potty trained, a good chance).

We isolate our pup for between 2 to 20 min or until calm. Say 2 min minimum until age 3 months, and longer if older. Just note the following points so that it's both effective and safe:

- When we *calmly* lead our pup into isolation, we don't speak, we don't touch our pup, and we don't look at it either.

- Note that all dogs, unless traumatized, understand our body language much better than our words, so we must really take care not to communicate our current feelings through our gestures or movements

- We don't let our pup out when it whines or barks (it will!) - Door scratchguards (mygermanshepherd.org/go/door-scratchguard) can help if our pup likes to scratch on the door behind which we disappeared; also note that as long as our pup whines or barks, it isn't making any trouble in that room - maybe this can help you to keep cool and control ;-)

- If not calm after 20 min, we take a bowl of water (mygermanshepherd.org/go/spill-proof-dog-tra vel-bowl) inside that safe room (again, note the procedure written above; we simply put down the water bowl and leave)

- If needed, every 20 min we pretend to only want to fill up the water

- We continue this isolation until our puppy is totally calm - don't worry, all puppies get the message, some sooner, others a bit later: Puppies require a lot of patience

- We only let our puppy out once calm for a couple of minutes - or when Isolation exceeds 90 min

- Then, again we don't speak, we don't touch our pup, and we don't look at it either, we simply open the door to the safe room and then go back to do what we were doing

The first few times, our pup will now seek our attention - and we do what we saw under Puppy Attention Seeking (p~98), ie we will continue to **ignore** our puppy just for a bit.

This is crucial because only in this moment (when *out*):

- Our pup builds an understanding that its behavior wasn't what we wanted

- And somehow it is 'saving a marker' in memory that seems to prevent repetition (immediately or soon, exactly like with the Collar Freeze above, p~142).

Then after a few minutes, when we have finished doing whatever we wanted to do, we call our puppy to us and *now* we give our attention and affection.

With a young puppy, this is probably a good time to go for a walk - particularly if isolation exceeded 60 min, and regardless whether our pup did its business on the indoor potty (mygermanshepherd.org/go/ugodog).

Why? Because a walk is wonderfully distracting - which is what we want, now that our pup 'got the message'.

Conclusion:

The NO-Force, NO-Fear, NO-Fuss Puppy Training doesn't need force, fear, food treats, shouting, electronic devices, or physical restraints - it *only* needs the **Collar Freeze** (we freeze, not our dog) and **Isolation** (while we look after our dog).

Can you imagine that it nonetheless works better than all other training approaches?

Try it out, apply The NO-Force, NO-Fear, NO-Fuss Puppy Training FROM TODAY, and be amazed yourself, and amaze your puppy!

But we are not done just yet. Because, we don't just want to train and develop our puppy and become its *accepted* Pack leader, we want more! After all, that's why dog lovers like us get a dog or a puppy, right?

We want to have a **great relationship** with our dog. A bonding that goes beyond having an *obedient* dog.

In fact, all the fuss about **Obedience Training** I personally consider as ... 'rubbish' (sorry). In this regard you may of course feel different but for me with my liberal mind, an 'obedient' family member is not what I want from a domesticated dog.

For me, a *machine* must be 'obedient', but not a living being - whether humane or canine. I make mi*n*takes, I don't want a dog obedient to a moron like me.

How to Best Socialize a Puppy

The purpose of **socializing** our puppy is to confront our dog from early on with different situations and environments that it is likely to encounter throughout its life.

The reason for an *early* encounter is twofold:

- While our dog is still young and new to us, we are much more likely to pay close attention and to *gently* introduce our puppy to new stimuli. Also, we do not yet *expect* our pup to react the way we want (which, later on, we often do!)

- The younger the dog and the newer the stimulus, the more we can shape our dog's future behavior towards it (explained subsequently).

As indicated under Family Socialization (p~66), during the four weeks between age 8 weeks and age 3 months puppies are most receptive to the stimuli we provide in the family pack.

See this as the natural *complement* of what the puppy learned during Litter Socialization (p~65) - because that's what it is. The first four weeks with us need to *add* all the behavior training elements that the dog pack couldn't provide during the first 8 weeks of our pup's life.

The first four weeks of **Family Socialization** will substantially influence our dog's future behavior, and how well our dog integrates with our family.

Like with humans, until this age - so before Puberty (p~68) - the neurons in the brain form most of the connections that determine intelligence, attitude, and future behavior (called *facilitation*). This is why it is much easier to shape the dog's behavior when we get the dog as a puppy.

Nonetheless, *some* neuronal connections continue to form throughout until old age (the older, the less). This is why it is still possible to shape the behavior of an older dog. It then just requires much more consistent repetition to achieve facilitation.

This means: As long as you are willing to provide the right amount of the *right* training, there is no problem if you don't get your puppy at age 8 weeks, or indeed if you don't get a puppy at all but instead an adult dog.

But I would argue that the first four weeks with us *always* significantly shape the future behavior of our dog, *regardless* at what age we get our new dog. This is because obviously *new* neuronal connections are primarily (if not only) formed when *new* stimuli have to be processed.

This storm of new stimuli is wildest during the first few weeks when we have a new dog. Everything is new to our dog: We are new, and how we behave, smell, speak, and look at our dog, as well as all the environment in our house and outside!

Therefore, how we present ourselves during the first four weeks, and what situations and environments we present to our new dog, will significantly influence how well our dog will integrate into its new family pack.

That's why I indicated already under Family Socialization (p~66) above that we must intensely **socialize** our new puppy and systematically expose it to a broad variety of noises, sights, smells, animals, humans, and situations, so that our pup will not *fear* any of these in the future. Yes, not even be *irritated* by any of these in the future.

Whether it's a screaming child that runs past our puppy, or a noisy motorbike, or a galloping horse, or anything else.

The most successful socialization of our new puppy is to somewhat *systematically* expose our pup to a broad array of environments, right from the first day when we get our dog. This is much better than going through a *book-long* 'Socialization Checklist'.

Accordingly, in the chapter 'Puppy Development Little Helpers' a bit later in this book you will find a *model* socialization schedule.

Meaning, you can divert from it as much as you like, it's only an *example* - but one that would ensure that you systematically cover all areas that are important for your puppy's development.

Just note that socializing our puppy for a specific stimulus in *one* situation or environment does not necessarily mean that our pup is now well socialized *regardless* of the situation and environment.

This is because as early as age 3 months many puppies will notice the slightest difference in situation or environment. Any change, and they may consider the entire experience as new - which may require a new round of socializations that involve the specific stimulus.

Basically, there exist two possible goals when we go about socializing our dog:

- Either we want our pup to *remain calm* (be unconcerned, no fear, and no irritation)

- Or we want our pup to boldly *intervene* (in a certain way that we find desirable)

How to Train Our Puppy to Remain Calm

Again, best is that we *ignore* our puppy when it reacts to something we don't want it to react to (see Puppy Attention Seeking, p~98). The goal here is to lower our pup's energy level.

This really is an incredibly powerful and gentle approach that we should always remember! Too many dog lovers regularly forget that puppies are *not* children (although we may often like to see it that way).

When we pay no attention when some stimulus makes our puppy jumpy, then we effectively *demonstrate* to our pup that we remain calm ourselves, despite the stimulus.

Canines learn much more from
our body language
than from anything we could say or do!

When we show *indifference* about the stimulus ourselves, then our pup will soon assume the same indifference and *relax*, despite the stimulus.

This is because of the intense Pack orientation of dogs - see The Right Mindset (p~60), The Prime

Secret about Dogs (p~88), and Puppy Attention Seeking (p~98). If we only let them, dogs are great at imitating our own energy level.

Never forget that a puppy has an inherent desire to *please* its Pack members. All the more once we are the *accepted* Pack leader.

Besides ignoring, the *next* best training approach would appear to be one that you probably prefer. And I, and every other dog lover too. But this approach is already limited to certain stimuli only:

If a particular situation or environment makes our puppy *fearful*, then we can choose to *comfort* our pup, instead of demonstratively *ignoring* the stimulus.

Examples: thunderstorm, firecrackers, or approaching aggressive dog.

However, this approach is not only limited to stimuli that may create *fear*, it also bears significant problems:

Even if we don't tremble, our **body language** will almost certainly reveal a raised energy level (and the fact of *comforting* our pup alone demonstrates this). The raised energy level signals our pup "My pack buddy/pack leader is worried about this too!" - even if we are not.

That's why this approach almost never works. Although it *appears* to be very considerate, it does *not* actually help our pup in such way that our pup remains unconcerned when the same stimulus appears the next time. Quite the opposite: This makes it likely that our dog then seeks our comforting intervention indefinitely!

So, whenever we want our puppy to remain unconcerned about a specific stimulus, best is that we behave unconcerned ourselves.

Momentarily this can be hard at times, but the indefinite payoff is worth it!

- If our puppy is on the Short Leash (mygermansh epherd.org/go/teaching-lead), we may lead our pup a bit further away from the stimulus and do some SSCD (p~116). This helps to distract and calm down both, us *and* our dog.

- If our puppy is not on the leash, we may perform the Collar Freeze (p~142).

- However, typically we will *not* isolate our puppy, because we can only demonstrate that we are unconcerned about the stimulus while our pup can *see* us.

But what do most dog owners do? - They try to "shush" their dog quiet ("shush, shush, shush") or lock it away!

As you see here, both is counter-productive. And the reason is what I just wrote above - a fact that can't be repeated often enough:

**Canines learn much more from
our body language
than from anything we could say or do!**

How to Train Our Puppy to Intervene

The typical situation where we would probably want to see that our dog would *intervene* if it happens in the future is when we are being attacked (even if we have a toy breed dog, because their small bite can hurt enormously).

The 'problem' here is that if our Family Socialization (p~66) was somewhat 'successful' then already with or before Puberty (p~68) our puppy may be able to notice very well whether we are *really* being attacked or whether we fake it.

Although canines are not good at reading intent (*pretend* to throw a ball, and most dogs run several meters before they realize that you haven't thrown anything), canines are typically excellent at reading our emotional state.

After all, that's what they have been bred for, over thousands of years: to focus on what we might want (in other words, to *please* us).

Our emotional state is of course very different once we are *really* being attacked (that's why Protection Dog Training follows a different approach, but that's another matter).

So how do we prepare our puppy for a situation where we expect it to *intervene*, but where our emotional state is less significant? How do we socialize our pup for this - if we want to?

I personally can't even think of any other situation where we would want our puppy to intervene(?), so better consider this chapter just for the purpose of completeness.

Whenever we want our puppy to *intervene* upon the occurrence of a certain stimulus, we must raise its energy level.

Just be aware that a higher energy level makes the situation or environment more memorable for our dog. This is a side effect we may not always want (however, this is of great help to heal a traumatized dog, but that's another matter as well).

Because of the canine quest number 1(!), to secure food (see The Prime Secret about Dogs, p~88), we could involve a very tasty food treat.

However, to combine a raised energy level with food always is a bad idea, because this triggers **food aggression** - plus, it may quickly have negative health implications, like Vomiting (mygermansheph erd.org/my-german-shepherd/german-shepherd-hea lth/german-shepherd-vomiting - again, note that all links are relevant to your puppy regardless of breed or mix!), Diarrhea (mygermanshepherd.org/my-ger man-shepherd/german-shepherd-health/german-she pherd-diarrhea), Bloat and Gastric Torsion (mygermanshepherd.org/my-german-shepherd/germansh epherd-health/german-shepherd-bloat-or-gastric-torsion).

But canine quest number 2, to belong to a Pack, helps here: To train our puppy to intervene, we should first position ourselves in such way that the instigating stimulus is closer to us than to our puppy, ideally even *separates* us from our puppy:

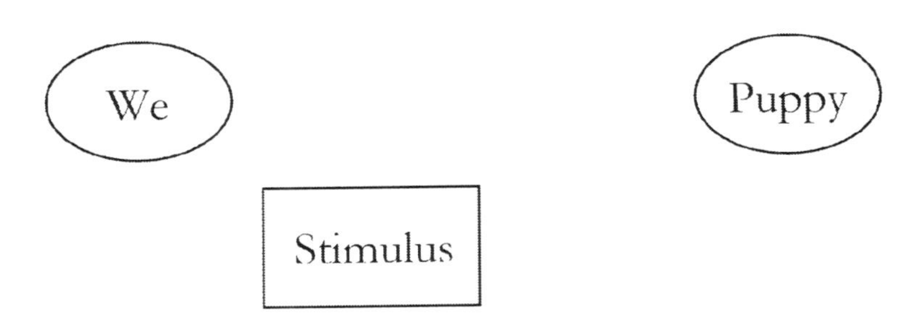

Now we can be pretty sure that our pup will do whatever it can to 'protect' us from that stimulus - *whether or not* we are already the accepted Pack leader (that's the interesting point!). Even at an age before puppies typically start to strive for Pack *leadership* (see Puberty, p~68), they already have a strong focus on Pack *membership*.

That's why already very young pups are often so fierceful when anything intrudes their perceived Pack (even if say the 'intruder' is on the other side of the street and on the leash!).

Puppies are not rational, their behavior is not based on rationality. Puppy behavior is based on hereditary traits.

If the setting of the socialization situation is not enough, then we would need to additionally motivate our pup to intervene by way of agitated body movements (waving arms, running) and/or excitement in our voice.

Bite Inhibition Training

Another key factor of socializing our puppy is Bite Inhibition Training. The term was coined by Ian Dunbar in his book After you get your puppy (mygermanshepherd.org/go/book-after-you-get-your-puppy).

Bite Inhibition means:

- to limit the occurrence of biting, and
- to limit the bite force when bitten.

If we want to raise our pup to become a protection dog, we will only aim for the first point above. But in all other cases we must address both points - or we, our children, other people or other animals may be in danger when our dog is grown up and much stronger!

There are many ways how we can teach our puppy **Bite Inhibition**, and we should start this from the day we take our pup home, and continue it until our dog becomes a senior dog (yes!).

Best ways to train our puppy Bite Inhibition:

- Briefly taking away the food bowl
- Briefly interrupting meals to add a tasty morsel
- Hand-feeding morsels

- Taking away a bone, chew toy, and other toys *from the mouth*

- Play-fighting (with frequent controlled interruptions!)

- Toothbrushing and mouth inspection

All of these measures train our puppy to use its mouth responsibly (similar to what mum and litter mates did during Litter Socialization, p~65).

When used consistently, these measures train our pup both:

- to consciously limit occurrence of biting and bite force

- and to subconsciously develop a modified bite reflex.

This is beneficial and important because it's our only guarantee during our dog's adult life later, that not even a **bite reflex** in shock or pain can injure us.

Good Bite Inhibition Training will in almost all cases prevent serious injury no matter how strong our dog's jaws later are. In the vast majority of cases good Bite Inhibition Training will actually prevent any laceration at all: The 'bite' won't break the skin. Meaning there's no risk of infection either.

Most important of all the above measures is the food-related Bite Inhibition Training (because it addresses the prime canine quest, see Combining the Feeding Routine with Bite Inhibition Training, p~111), and the training during play-fighting as described in the following chapter (because that's puppies' prime activity during a major part of puppyhood).

The Importance of Puppy l
Play-Fighting

The major part of all puppy behavior is Play, and the major part of all Puppy Play is Play-fighting

Note that this is entirely *natural* puppy behavior, so nothing to worry about (instead, it would be worrying if your pup *doesn't* want to play-fight with you).

So we must **not** curb this puppy behavior because it allows us to get the dog we want: Foremost, a dog that's *safe* for us and others!

BUT: During any Play and Play-fighting with our pup we *must* frequently interrupt the play, so that our puppy learns that we are in control at all times, no matter how excited or worked out our dog is:

- Every minute (max), we will interrupt Play and ask our pup to SIT or lie DOWN (literally to *relax*). Only if complied with our visual cue or vocal command, after a few *seconds* we will continue playing.
- Similarly, when our pup nips (p~243) us a tad too strong, we will also interrupt Play to sym-

...bolically 'take care of our wounds' - while our pup either has to lie down or may 'comfort' us in apology. Again, only if complied, after half a *minute* (up to a minute) we will continue playing.

Note that the interruption upon nipping should be considerably longer than our ordinary interruption of Play, so that our pup learns that it did something wrong.

This Bite Inhibition Training during Play-fighting with us should by all means be complemented by Play-fighting with other people (friends, relatives) and other animals (dogs, and maybe cats) wherever possible. So that our puppy learns to inhibit its bite force not only towards family members but towards all people and other animals as well.

However, note that the popular tug-of-war should be excluded from Play-fighting until the adult teeth have firmly replaced all baby teeth (which normally is not before age 7 or even 8 months). If you play tug-of-war with your pup any sooner, you risk gum and tooth problems that may require extra vet visits that can cost hundreds to thousands of dollars.

This is the reason for avoiding tug-of-war, *not* behavioral consequences as you can read so often. If you play *right*, like described here, tug-of-war is excellent play.

Training Consistency

Another key factor of the *right* puppy training is of course consistency.

'Of course'?

Why is it then so widespread that dog owner families are so *inconsistent* in their whole training approach? Not just between different family members but even the same family member at different times?

- What dog commands they give, how they give them, what they mean with each command, what puppy behavior they expect as a result, etc.
- When they feed, what they feed, how much they feed, the feeding routine they employ, etc.
- When they take the puppy for a walk, how they take the pup for a walk, and how they control and treat the pup once outside, etc.

Inconsistency is highly irritating for a puppy. Feeling irritated causes stress. This stress further *increases* the conflict the pup is experiencing in its 'pack'. And, to close the circle, this stress leads to health and behavior problems.

So, we don't let it come so far! We show consistent behavior to our pup, and we have consistent expectations as to its own behavior.

The 'Puppy Development Little Helpers' in the next chapter can help with this.

Puppy Development Little Helpers

To help us with our own puppy development and puppy training here, you may want to make use of the subsequent 'little Helpers'. Or feel free to develop your own.

Simplicity is best!

If you print out these forms, you can easily fill them in multiple times, tick off the points done or achieved, and you can take the relevant Little Helpers always with you.

Commands Little Helper

All command training must be clear, concise, and consistent. We ensure that everyone in the family uses the same command to achieve the same behavior from our pup.

That's why we **write them down** and say, stick them on the fridge - these dog magnets (mygermanshepherd.org/go/paw-print-magnets) are great to continue to notice the Little Helpers on the fridge door:

Command	Meaning
Example: Verbal cue: "SIT" Visual cue:	Buttocks on the ground, but front feet standing

Feeding Routine Little Helper

The Feeding Routine (p~104) we employ for our puppy has a fundamental impact on our dog's **well-being and behavior** (see The Prime Secret about Dogs, p~88).

So it makes sense to take a few notes for this too:

Week	Gesture Eating/ Pup complied	Basic Diet Description	Symptoms? Allergies? Feces? Behavior? Calm?

Leash Training Little Helper

Another important area of our puppy development is Leash Training (p~113; also revisit How to Become the *Accepted* Pack Leader, p~96). Here's a Little Helper for that:

Week	Loose Leash Walk?	Unleashed Heel?	Recall successful environments?

Socialization Little Helper

In the chapter How to Best Socialize a Puppy (p~150) you saw why we should try to expose our puppy during the first four weeks to as many different environments as we can, and how to proceed.

Here's the corresponding Little Helper. Tick off once your pup *remains calm* (or, where marked, *intervenes* the way you want). No need for a timeline, just try to provide as many experiences as possible during the first 4 weeks.

Nonetheless, getting the behavior right should have absolute priority over the sheer *number* of socialization situations that you feel you can 'tick off'.

Exposure to:	Tick off
Feelings	
Family members hugging	
Family members kissing ...	
Family member being 'attacked' - pup should intervene	
Family member lying on the ground, below dog's line of vision	
Long eye contact with all family members	
Moments when family members are angry	
Moments when family members are pleased	
Moments when family members are totally calm	
Moments when family members are excited	
Moments when other people are angry	
Moments when other people are excited	
A congregation of dogs (say in a dog park)	
An aggressive dog passing by	
The woods, the sea (ideally), wild terrain, busy streets	
Halloween or other party	
Vet visit	
Different surfaces while walking (grass, gravel, asphalt,...)	

Exposure to:	Tick off
Smells	
Kitchen smells, incl cooking meat	
Dog Blanket smell after washing (and proper rinsing!)	
Smell of all family clothes when worn, incl leather	
Smell of all family clothes when washed	
House cleaning agents - should put pup off!	
Sounds	
Vacuum cleaner	
Nearby motorbikes	
Nearby gunshots (certainly if Protection Dog)	
Children's noises (yelling, screaming, playing; say at school)	
Baby crying from inside a rolling and shaking pram	
People having a loud argument	
Nearby airplane and helicopter	
Thunderstorm (ideally) and fireworks (but not too close!)	
Breaking ocean waves (ideally)	
Sounds of different horns and siren	
Snoring (if relevant)	
Rewing engines	
Howling wind	
People applauding	
Radio voices and music	

Exposure to:	**Tick off**
<u>Sights</u>	
People dressed (entirely) in black, white, yellow, and blue	
People wearing large hats, scarves, turban, gloves, sunglasses	
People wearing motorbike helmet	
People wearing a beard	
People with umbrella and raincoat	
People wearing clunky leather gear and in uniform	
People wearing clogs, flip flops, boots, etc	
TV	
<u>Movements</u>	
Children running past	
Joggers, skaters and cyclists rushing past	
Motorbikes and horses riding past	
Cats, rabbit, ducks, swan, cows	
Large vans, buses, trucks	
Rides in different cars	
Air travel and boat travel (if you anticipate it to happen)	
Running along your bicycle, on-leash and off-leash	
People in wheelchairs and on crutches	
Falling snow (where relevant)	
Door banged shut by draft	

Behavior Modification Little Helper

In the chapter The ONLY 'Punishment' You'll Ever Need (p~138) you saw that where the famous dog trainers use:

- force
- fear
- food treats (lots of/systematic)
- raised voice (shouting)
- electronic devices
- physical restraints

instead, we only need the Collar Freeze (p~142) and Isolation (p~145) as *gentle* and *animal pack like* means of behavior modification.

Apart from this, we heavily rely on motivational behavior (p~19) and we use Rewards (p~132), but not food treats. And when a puppy or adult dog is on the leash anyway then we might do a bit of SSCD (p~116). That's all!

In case you struggle to take all of this in, here's the final Little Helper:

Week	Isolations? Why? How long?	Collar Freeze? Why? How long?	SSCD? How long?	Rewards How given? Favorite?

House Training a Puppy

House Training is another BIG topic that belongs to **Puppy Development and Puppy 101**.

House training comprises much more than just housebreaking (potty training, toilet training).

House training comprises ALL training our puppy needs in order to behave well in the house. So that we can let our dog loose in the house, without having to fear:

- Potty accidents
- Scratched furniture
- Torn carpets or our favorite Persian rug disintegrating
- Our Chinese vase being knocked over
- Our slippers or Gucci shoes chewed to bits
- The grilled turkey miraculously disappearing from the kitchen counter
- Dog begging besides the dinner table
- Dog hair in our bed
- Our bed duvet in our dog's crate

- Our child being bitten or scratched
- Our cat being chased
- Our couch being taken in possession
- etc.

It is for these reasons why some dog owners keep their puppy in an indoor *cage* crate (like you saw at the beginning of the book), and their adult dog in an outdoor kennel.

That is not what our modern domesticated dogs have been bred for. Domesticated means 'made for the house', where we live ourselves (domus is Latin, and means house). We don't live in a cage, do we?

Of course dog owners can choose where they want to keep their dog (within reason), but my point is:

All dog lovers who keep their dog locked away only do so out of *fear* - that things could happen like the ones listed above. And this fear is unjustified if only we apply the *right* puppy training from the outset, like you find it in this book.

Accordingly, let's briefly address all the above points in this book, but in order.

Puppy House Training comprises:

- Puppy Meals - to such degree that they don't lead to Vomiting (mygermanshepherd.org/my-german-shepherd/german-shepherd-health/german-shepherd-vomiting/) or Diarrhea (mygermanshepherd.org/my-german-shepherd/german-shepherd-health/german-shepherd-diarrhea)

- Puppy Meal Times (to such degree that they promote regular potty times)

- Puppy Feeding Routine (p~104)

- Puppy Housebreaking (potty training, toilet training)

- Puppy Crate Training

- Puppy Leash Training (has to start *inside* the house, p~113)

- Puppy Behavior Training (instead of medieval Obedience Training, has to start *inside* the house)

Puppy Food

The Dog food industry makes us believe that puppies (like senior dogs) would need a special diet that matches their development, because different stages of development would mean different nutritional needs.

But this is not true. After weaning, puppies do NOT need a special diet, a diet other than adult dogs need. Wild dog puppies and wolf puppies also get exactly the same food as their parents! And they thrive on it, and become the next generation of parents. Very successfully. For thousands of years.

The only reason why the dog food industry makes us believe that puppies need a special puppy diet is that the dog food industry needs more of our money (well, *wants* more of our money). More product variety means more chances to find buyers. It really is that simple. It is just about economics, not about puppy development.

But note my words above: Puppies do not need a diet other than what adult dogs *need* - not what adult dogs typically *get*: Kibble or tinned food (crap) full of fillers, chemical emulsifiers, color and flavor additives, hormones, antibiotics, and other chemicals. *Specifically* made that way by the dog food industry.

That is not what puppies need. And that is not what adult dogs need either.

In fact, another problem specifically with the industrial puppy foods is the incredible *imbalance* of nutrients: far too much artificially added proteins, grains, and vitamin and mineral supplements.

What is *sold* as being healthy, actually leads to the widespread gastrointestinal complications, bone diseases, and ailments reaching as far as Arthritis (mygermanshepherd.org/my-german-shepherd/german-shepherd-health/german-shepherd-arthritis) and Obesity (mygermanshepherd.org/my-german-shepherd/german-shepherd-health/german-shepherd-obesity).

Of course, the dog food industry wants you to believe that your puppy would benefit from their nutrition-enrichment exercises, but come on: What can be more beneficial to your puppy than getting just a good mix of naturally occurring foods?

There is nothing healthier for puppies than a standard *balanced* diet that has similarities with the wild dog diet:

The Wild Dog Diet

The diet of wild dogs consists of about 75% meat, bone, and innards such as tripe, liver etc, and 25% greens like grasses, twigs, leaves, dandelion, chard, apples, pears, berries, parsley, kale, parsnip, yam, squash, etc.

There is no need to treat your puppy like a wild dog or ancient wolf and give it the wild dog diet. But likewise, there is no need to treat your puppy like a guinea pig and give it foods it neither needs nor benefits from!

However, there *is* a need to give your puppy a healthy diet that is *balanced* and nutrition-rich. Nutrition-rich not as in 'enriched' or 'fortified' with additives, no, just a good variety of standard natural food. Because this *does* comprise all the nutrition necessary and beneficial to your puppy.

Ingredients of a Healthy Puppy Diet

- Meats like beef, pork, lamb, venison, or even lean bacon

- Poultry like turkey or chicken breast

- Innards like liver sausage

- Vegetables like cabbage, kale, lettuce, carrots, cucumber, celery, broccoli, spinach, sugar snaps, etc

- Fruits like pumpkin, strawberries, blueberries, raspberries, orange, clementine, nectarine, apple, banana, watermelon, cantaloupe, etc

- Dairies like milk, scrambled eggs, and reduced-fat cheese

- Fish like (boneless!) salmon and tuna
- Other foods like noodles and rice

By genetical heritage dogs are scavengers, thus their digestive system can process foods we wouldn't even consider as *food.*

Having lived on human food remains for thousands of years has changed the digestive system of dogs (from that of their ancestors, wolves) to one that can digest many human foods.

For example, today's dogs have 10 genes to digest starches and break down fats, and their actual activity in the Pancreas has been well documented. Thus the common advice to "avoid table scraps" actually is not so much for health reasons but for behavior reasons (mygermanshepherd.org/periodical/how-to-stop-scavenging).

However, the rise of commercial dog food (only as recently as the second half of the last century!) has led to dietary intoxication of practically all of today's dog breeds - with the result that now many dogs suffer from severe Digestive Disorders and their ramifications!

So, don't be surprised if your puppy cannot cope well with some of the foods you provide. The toy breed dogs are at particular risk.

This leads over to my final notes on the topic of Puppy Food.

Important points to note:

- Best is to give your puppy a homemade diet (mygermanshepherd.org/go/better-dog-meals). With practice, and preparing the food a week in advance and freezing it, this takes us no more than 45 min *a week* (so, 6 to 7 min per day)!

- Boiling, steaming, roasting etc will kill off almost all impurities and pathogens, and will make the food more digestible – but only steaming (mygermanshepherd.org/go/steamer) will retain its nutrients to a large degree.

- Always introduce new foods carefully, ie initially mix only a small amount of the new food into the current diet.

- A good rule is to introduce new foods with a spoonful only, *mixed under* the current diet. If digested well, for the next meal, replace a *quarter* of the current diet with the new foods, and each day or second day another quarter. If *not* digested well, return to the prior diet and introduce the new foods more slowly.

- IF you insist to feed your puppy commercial dog food nonetheless, then rotate through multiple dog food brands (mygermanshepherd.org/my-german-shepherd/mygermanshepherd-remedies/yummies) or try to mix their food for each meal (*very* important because of the nutritional *imbalance* of practically every dog food brand!)

- Absolutely crucial again is that you always provide a drinking bowl (mygermanshepherd.org/go/spill-proof-dog-travel-bowl) full of fresh water for your puppy to drink from at any time it feels like it. There is no excuse to limit your puppy's fresh water supply. Yes, your dog will need to go potty more often, but (s)he will be much healthier and calmer too (mygermanshepherd.org/my-german-shepherd/german-shepherd-health/german-shepherd-bladder-infection)

- In line with your puppy's development you will notice its need for *varying* amounts of food. Best is to start with *small* meals, and if your pup appears to remain hungry, give a bit more food at each meal-time.

Note that since we are dog lovers, it is impossible that we feed too little. So don't worry, just don't feed too much. ;-)

Puppy Meal Times

As explained in Puppy Feeding Routine (p~104), best is to give our puppy *three* or even *four* meals a day.

Obviously, these meals should be well spread out over the entire day. However, there are some issues to consider:

- In the morning, our first task is to give our puppy a potty walk. No heavy exercise yet, just a walk.

- When we come back, we could then immediately give our pup the first small meal (breakfast so to say).

- But I prefer to run two or three early morning training sessions beforehand, see Right Time for Puppy Training (p~81). In other words, our pup won't have its first meal before an hour into the new day. If we get up at 7, this means around 8.

- Similarly, the last meal in a day is restricted too. Say, our pup's crate time starts at 10 in the evening, then we won't feed anything after 8 or 8.30. And just before crate time there is a short and calming potty walk.

- This means, we have to fit in one or two further puppy meals during the 12 hours of the day.

- If you plan to feed three meals, I'd suggest to give the third meal right in the middle of that, around 2pm.

- If you plan to feed four meals, I'd suggest to give a smaller meal around 12, and another smaller meal around 4pm.

- Within reason, it doesn't really matter which exact meal times you choose. What matters is that you aim to feed your puppy always at the same times (consistency). Because this is better for both health *and* behavior reasons.

- If you forget a meal (happens!), stick to the same meal times nonetheless, but give a bit more food for the next upcoming meal (but not twice the amount).

- At each meal time, provide a full water bowl (mygermanshepherd.org/go/spill-proof-dog-travel-bowl) about 50 inches apart.

- Within a week or two you will have found out which **meal times** are best for your pup in terms of behavior, potty going, and sleeping.

Puppy Feeding Routine

Puppy Feeding Routine we have already discussed where it belongs (namely as a means we *must* use to reduce the conflict our pup is experiencing in its Pack).

See Puppy Feeding Routine (p~104).

8 Secrets to Housebreaking a Puppy in 7 Days or Less

For most dog owners, housebreaking a puppy (potty training, toilet training) possibly is the most annoying part of having a puppy.

Nonetheless, puppy housebreaking need not be as difficult as some people make it appear. After all, a puppy has not yet developed a routine when and where to go potty, which means we don't need to *break* an existing routine. Instead, if we do it right, we can fairly easily train our puppy to follow the routine we want, even at the times we want - within limits.

However, we must be consistent and patient. It can take up to a week before our puppy is housebroken, meaning clean in the house. That is IF we do it right. If we *don't* do it right, then our pup may need many weeks or even months before it is housebroken.

So, how do we do it *right*, such that we will hardly need the mop at all?

1. Walk your puppy frequently and regularly (every 60 min until about age three months, at night every 2 hours; for reasons see Right Time for Puppy Training, p~81). - If you can't, you will need to provide a potty training pad (my-germanshepherd.org/go/pads) or puppy potty (mygermanshepherd.org/go/pet-toilet-turf) which you place at the main door.

Note that *regularly* is crucial: Only if you walk your puppy at the *same times* during the day and night, the pup's metabolism and subconsciousness can adapt to your rhythm, and urinate and defecate 'on command' (because basically that is what you require from the dog when you expect the dog to relieve during the few minutes you are dog-walking, right?!)

2. Ensure that your puppy cannot run free in the house before (s)he is housebroken. That does **not** mean you should lock your dog in a cage-style kennel (like this: mygermanshepherd.org /go/metal-cage-crate). Instead, better keep your pup in a tiled room in the first few weeks (one or two weeks more than you feel is needed - just to be safe).

3. When you weren't fast enough to take your puppy for a short walk or to let it in the garden (or to ensure it hits the dog potty), you will need to clean the affected area thoroughly or else your pup will be attracted to that 'potty area' going forward!

A good and cheap solution is to buy a bottle of concentrated vinegar (the clear one that's also brilliant to descale your kettle: mygermanshepherd.org/go/concentrated-vinegar). Mix an equal amount of water and vinegar, and give the affected area a final wipe-down with this solution. Do not let your fingers contact the concentrated vinegar solution (it 'burns').

There is no need to buy the (alcohol-based!) Nature's Miracle Stain & Odor Remover (mygermanshepherd.org/go/natures-miracle-stain-and-odo r-remover) - but if you prefer alcohol, in this case it does the job too. ;-)

4. To avoid having to do this often (or at all), in addition to the frequent and *regular* potty walks (see 1), do observe your puppy very closely during the first week: Try to detect the typical body language just before (s)he needs to relieve (*every* dog reveals its unique potty signals, even the *urgency*)

I found that this is *much easier* when we habitually film the pup during the first week (is a lovely keepsake anyway): A small digital camera (mygermanshepherd.org/go/digital-camera) with movie function (set to lowest resolution for long footage) on a tripod (mygermanshepherd.org/go/camera-tripod) or a good webcam with autofocus (mygermanshepherd.org/go/webcam) that broadly captures our dog's typical place is sufficient. Stop the recording the moment before you leave for the dog walk, and turn it back on after you come home.

In the evening, use fast forward to quickly review the 2 min before each walk. After two days (max) you should be able to identify your pup's unique potty signals that indicate that (s)he needs to relieve. Bang! Now puppy housebreaking is a snap!

Going forward, watch out for this behavior and when you notice it, make a turbo run through the subsequent potty routine and take your puppy out (sticking to the routine even if rushed is better! Just leave out steps b) and c) below).

5. Right from the start, tie the short leash (mygermanshepherd.org/go/teaching-lead) to the main door handle, and let a small bell (mygermanshepherd.org/go/mini-bell) dangle down to your pup's height.

a) 10 to 15 minutes before you take your puppy for a walk, let your pup watch you while you take down the short leash from the door handle, and attach the leash to your pup's collar

b) Now let your puppy run around in the house with the leash attached (see Short Leash Training, p~122)

c) 2 to 5 minutes before you go for the walk, do some SSCD

d) Before you leave the house, motivate your pup to push against the bell (or do it yourself)

e) You go through the door first, your pup stays behind you - if your pup tries to get out first, close the door and do some more SSCD

This procedure will help your puppy to soon build a mental connection between: leash - indoor walk - SSCD - being completely calm - bell - door - staying behind you - being taken for a walk - and relieving! Before you know it, your pup will nudge the bell to your delight.

6. Always use the same vocal and visual cue when you want to signal your pup when and where to go potty. This will help your puppy to develop a potty routine more quickly.

7. Do <u>not</u> reward your pup with a Food Treat for expected routine behavior like going potty. Otherwise you disturb the whole training concept of puppy meals, meal times, and feeding routine. Expected routine behavior should always only be rewarded with Praise. Even Affection we save for *non-routine* <u>behavior we desire</u>.

8. Only use motivation (ie the above **behavior-training** elements), not punishment in your dog training. Eg never dip your pup's nose in the urine or something like that. That's not only sick, it's also unwise because it doesn't teach your puppy a thing while it will definitely harm your relationship with your dog and seed future dog aggression too!

If you get these eight points right from the start, then you will see that you can *actually* manage house-breaking your puppy within a week (max!).

Do we need to meticulously record our puppy's food and water intake (as so often recommended)?

No. *Regular* potty walks (see 1) and identifying your pup's unique potty signals from the film footage (see 4) - and of course to avoid scavenging - is *much more* reliable to avoid accidents!

For the reasons detailed earlier ('flush the bladder' to prevent Bladder Infections: mygermanshep-herd.org/ my-german-shepherd/german-shepherd-health/ger man-shepherd-bladder-infection), pup-pies *must* have free access to water all day and night (and I don't waste my time to measure how much I fill in).

Puppy Crate Training

Crate training means to make our puppy use its crate *voluntarily* as its primary domicile for sleeping, dozing, playing with a toy (particularly chew toy: mygermanshepherd.org/go/dog-chew-toys-hurley), and when feeling unwell. Just like children would primarily use their room when they play indoors or when they sleep.

The *right* crate training is crucial for a great relationship with our dog. A properly crate-trained puppy will require *much* less behavior training:

- Once our puppy uses its crate *voluntarily*, this will significantly reduce **whining**, **barking**, **separation anxiety**, **aggression**, and **destructive behaviour**!
- In addition it helps to prevent that our adult dog is later taking possession of our bed, our couch, or our favorite armchair.

From the chapter Prepare a Place to Rest and Sleep (p~43) we know already which features the crate should have, and where to place it in the house.

10 Most Common Mistakes When Crate Training

To me it's no surprise that so many dogs don't use their crate *voluntarily*. Because dog owners add element after element to a long chain of mistakes:

1. They are *not considerate* about the crate - the small space which the puppy should be allowed to treat as its own. They pull out the blanket while the pup is in the crate, or they step into its crate, or they apply force to get the puppy into the crate or out of it, etc. - NO. Both puppy *and* owner will need to learn how to use the crate.

2. They use *many food treats* to get their pup into the crate, to make their pup sit down, and to make their pup lie down in its crate. - NO. Any food treat at the crate should be limited to the first time: If it's necessary to motivate the puppy to experience the inside of the crate at all (only exception: putting a food treat inside a Treat Toy (mygermanshepherd.org/go/dog-treat-toys-tux), but even this is problematic because your pup may want to come to get it filled up again).

3. They put *many* toys in the crate. - NO. Always provide just *one* toy at a time (plus one chew toy, that's okay).

4. They *interact* with the puppy at its crate. - NO. While at the crate, only *talk* once a while in a calm tone to make your puppy calm too.

5. They combine Crate Training with Behavior Training (p~209) to make the puppy go into its crate, then sit, and then lie down. - NO. Whatever happens at your puppy's crate must happen because of your pup's own will!

6. They make their puppy *excited* at the crate. - NO. Even when your pup stayed in its crate for a minute for the first time and you go back to the crate to praise your puppy, *don't* raise your voice to an excited level, because your energy level transfers to your pup.

7. They *reward* their puppy when it gets out of its crate - even when it followed them when they left the crate area. - NO. Never reward your pup when it gets out of its crate. The next couple of minutes no Praise, no Affection, no Toy, no Play, no nada.

8. They confine their pup to the crate just before they go out. - NO. Your puppy must not associate your 'being away' with 'having to stay in the crate'.

9. They have *exciting family action* going on (vocally or visibly) while they want their pup to remain in its crate. - NO. Obviously your puppy will want to join the family action, because your family is your pup's pack.

10. And, of course, many dog owners are *inconsistent* with their Crate Training.

To train our puppy to use its crate *voluntarily*, we must not make any of these mistakes.

10 Success Steps to Train a Puppy to Use its Crate Voluntarily

Although it's much more likely that your puppy will use the crate *voluntarily* if you have built it (as shown in Prepare a Place to Rest and Sleep, p~43), still there is no guarantee for this.

Also, accept the fact that it is inappropriate and unhealthy for dogs to be confined to a small crate area for hours during awake times. Even our modern domesticated dogs still have a hereditary *need* to run around a bit - or they *will* show behavior problems within one day and health problems within a week.

However, obviously there are times when we would love that our puppy stays in its crate *voluntarily* (that's the ideal). So, how can we promote this, that our puppy wants to use the crate - particularly at times when *we* want that?

1. It all starts with the right introduction to the crate. When we get our new puppy, we *show* it its crate, and we *motivate* our pup to get the feeling of being in the crate: We lead our puppy to the crate, and we wrap one food treat into the crate's extra blanket (see Prepare a Place to Rest and Sleep, p~43). Now we midly encourage our pup to search for the treat. While searching, our puppy will start to get used to being in the crate at all. That's it.

Note: If our pup pulls the blanket out of the crate to search for the treat, we calmly and quietly place the blanket back inside the crate. Dogs that pull their blanket out of the crate show us that they are missing an extra blanket where we are (its pack members).

We provide that extra resting place in every room where we want our dog to be with us, but the *crate blanket* we always place back inside the crate. It's a special 'crate blanket'.

2. During the first week, we will lead the way to the crate many times (ie we *don't* pull our pup on a lead to the crate or such thing!). Dogs learn best from our own behavior (our body language), not from commands, or even force!

Note: We never use the crate as a place for punishment or for our puppy to feel excluded. We only gently encourage our puppy *once* to *follow us* to the crate.

Also, once our puppy searched for the treat for the first time entirely inside its crate, we do *not* use Food treats anymore. Because this would set the wrong stimulus for expected routine behavior.

3. Instead, we put our puppy's seemingly favorite toy inside the crate (always only *one* toy at a time, plus one chew toy). We allow our pup to take the toy(s) out, but every so often we put them back in.

Note: Dogs must not have access to more than one toy at a time - plus one chew toy (mygermansheph erd.org/go/dog-chew-toys-hurley) if the toy itself is not a chew toy. Because dogs that feel that they can control access to their toys will not *accept* us as their Pack leader!

This is one of the many more situations that *increase* the conflict the dog is experiencing in its Pack - see The Prime Secret about Dogs (p~88) and How to Become the *Accepted* Pack Leader (p~96).

In addition, this is much safer: Only when we know which toy our puppy is currently having, we are able to notice say when it disintegrates and our pup is about to swallow small parts of it!

4. Every time when we come back from some exercise with our puppy, we wait a few minutes for our pup to calm down, and then we lead our pup to its crate. We remain nearby for a few minutes, and speak once a while in a calm tone to make our puppy calm too. But we *don't* interact with our pup at its crate.

Note: Initially, make sure to spend as much time at home as possible while your puppy is in the crate. Because, when you leave house, this is hard enough for your pup (see Separation Anxiety Cure: mygerm anshepherd.org/periodical/german-shepherd-dog-se paration-anxiety-cure), so by all means don't make your pup associate this negative experience with *having* to stay in its crate.

5. Whenever we are at the crate, and our puppy doesn't go inside voluntarily, we just stand there and wait (patience with puppies is crucial).

Note: If the current toy choice is not inside the crate, we place it back inside. If it is inside the crate but our pup doesn't go inside the crate for several minutes, obviously we haven't identified our pup's favorite toy (so we replace it right now).

6. If our puppy is not interested in any toy we provide in the crate, we gently take hold of our pup's collar and perform the Collar Freeze (p~142) to calm down our pup so much until it wants to lie down in its crate. In case this doesn't happen, we walk away and defer the crate training to later (ie we never enforce crate use).

Note: IF instead of building the crate yourself (mygermanshepherd.org/periodical/building-a-den-for-your-dog) you bought a commercial cage-style crate (a lockable kennel; mygermanshepherd.org/go/metal-cage-crate) that has a door, *don't* close the door initially. After a few minutes, leave the area where the crate is. Your puppy is likely to come after you. That's fine. Lead the way back to the crate several times - your pup will follow (as long as there is no negative association with the crate!).

7. We do not combine Crate Training with Behavior Training (p~209) or even Obedience Training: Giving commands at the crate leads to a negative association with crate time, which even impacts back on the success of the Behavior Training at all other places later!

Note: Instead, once our pup remains in its crate for one minute, we go back to the crate and reward our pup with *Praise* at its crate - *shortly* and *in a calm tone.* We don't make it get excited again.

One minute is plenty for a dog to disassociate prior experiences, which means it will now associate the *Praise* with being in the crate. That's exactly what we want for crate training our puppy.

We slowly extend the crate period before we would again go back to the crate and *shortly and calmly* reward our pup with Praise.

8. We never reward our puppy when it just got out of its crate.

Note: *None* of the 5 Reward Types (p~132). We don't even say things like "Oh, you little cutie, you should not come after me now" - because our typical 'sing song' tone we use with a puppy sounds like ... *Praise* to a dog, yes!

Any reward we give our pup when it gets out of its crate will make our puppy associate 'leaving the crate' with 'being rewarded', hence the opposite of what we want.

Once again: Never reward your puppy when it gets out of its crate. Instead, when you know that your pup is just coming from its crate, always wait a few minutes before you give *any* form of reward (and in this case, this includes giving Attention, see Reward Types, p~132). This is absolutely crucial for successful Crate Training!

9. Whenever we want our puppy to use its crate, obviously we don't engage with our puppy (play, praise, communicate, look) and we don't have excited family action going on - because then our pup will want to stay with us, not in its crate.

Note: You can enjoy your dog when you have guests (mygermanshepherd.org/periodical/enjoy-a-well-behaved-dog-when-you-have-guests) and even at such time make your puppy *want* to use its crate most of the time, if only you do it right (namely as described in this chapter).

Also, with consistency in your Crate Training approach, most puppies understand fairly quickly when you want them to stay in the crate, even if you did not close the crate door if it has one: Close the room's door to the crate area (you can leave it crack open so that your pup won't feel excluded from its Pack). Of course, if your pup then gets agitated, you first need to calm it down again.

10. Lastly, we are consistent with all the above points and show patience.

If you follow the steps above, particularly 4, 5, 7, and 8(!), then you'll see that after a few days your puppy will remain in the crate on its own choice for longer and longer periods, *and* many times even seek out the crate on its own initiative!

This is all *we* want from our own **Crate Training**, see the second paragraph in this chapter (p~200) about 'the fact we need to accept'.

Further notes:

- When you notice that your pup prefers a comfortable place elsewhere in the house (say on a pillow, blanket, or similar), although you are not even nearby, then this shows that (in your puppy's view) the crate is currently not comfortable enough. So, consider making changes (see Prepare a Place to Rest and Sleep, p~43).

- When your puppy barks or whines while in the crate (although you have not locked the door if it has one) then the barking or whining is not because your pup feels excluded from its Pack (it isn't). Then the barking or whining is Barking for Attention (p~225).

- The only exception: A traumatized dog may sometimes stay in an open (unlocked) crate and bark or whine for potty going, or because it is hungry or thirsty, or it feels in pain (then it will *whine* only).

- All non-traumatized dogs will in such cases get *out* of the crate and seek proximity to their owner.

- While feeling excluded from its Pack is a serious issue for dogs (for *why* see The Prime Secret about Dogs, p~88), not getting the desired attention is very different and not problematic at all (during Litter Socialization, p~65, all puppies experience this all the time). So, in such case we *ignore* the barking and whining (see Puppy Attention Seeking, p~98).

- Always place a drinking bowl (mygermansheph erd.org/go/spill-proof-dog-travel-bowl) full of fresh water near the crate.

Puppy Leash Training

Puppy Leash Training we have already discussed where it belongs (namely as a means we *must* use to reduce the conflict our pup is experiencing in its Pack).

See Puppy Leash Training (p~113).

Puppy Behavior Training

Puppy Behavior Training must start *inside* the house, therefore it can be considered part of **House Training** (House Training is by far the largest area of dog training, hence it is fully covered in House Training Dogs to Behave Well in a High Value Home).

Since too many people yet only **obedience-train** their dog, I will now make Puppy Behavior Training the last *main* chapter of this book.

Puppy Behavior Training

For most dog owners Puppy Behavior Training seems to end up as **behavior modification**, because they only start to think of Behavior Training *after* they are facing - what they call - 'puppy problems'.

Instead, of course Behavior Training should start before the first problems can arise, ie it should start on the same day we get our puppy. Ideally, **Behavior Training** will go hand in hand with **Obedience Training**, so that you don't *confuse* your pup with inconsistency - where your body language (mygermanshepherd.org/go/human-body-language) contradicts your verbal commands.

Thus, **Puppy Training** comprises basic command training and addressing the typical 'puppy problems', in particular:

- Puppy chewing
- Puppy scratching
- Puppy digging
- Puppy barking
- Puppy whining
- Puppy jumping

- Puppy mouthing, nipping, and biting
- Puppy aggression

So, let's close this book by addressing each of these areas of puppy behavior as well.

Puppy Chewing

Is your puppy chewing too much for your liking? Or just the wrong kind of items? Like your clothes, furniture, carpets, shoes, handbags, or whatever. Or maybe its own body parts, creating hot spots on its skin?

Never try to stop puppy chewing entirely because then you would promote early tooth loss and inflammation of the gums of your dog. Puppy chewing is a necessary period of your puppy growing up.

It can take anywhere between six to ten months for a pup's teeth to set into the jaw completely, which will make your pup chew on anything that gets in its way - unless you train your puppy from early on which items are tabu.

To prevent your puppy chewing on your favorite slippers, handbags, table legs etc, there are three main steps we can take:

1) Get at least three different chew toys that are suitable for your pup's bite strength and size of mouth. A great start is Westpaw's Hurley (mygermanshepherd.org/go/dog-chew-toys-hurley) and Nylabone's Galileo (mygermanshepherd. org/go/dog-chew-toys-nylabone-galileo).

When your pup then indeed chooses to chew on the provided chew toy, reward your pup immediately with Praise, Play, or Affection (no Food treat here).

2) When your puppy chews on items that are *tabu*, make use of suitable puppy training. You basically have two options:

- Either gently take the item away, use the most basic dog command (a sharp, short NO!), and do the Collar Freeze (p~142)

- Or use the situation to teach the 'LEAVE IT' command.

When we see (only then!) that our puppy is chewing on an item that it is not supposed to be chewing (say a shoe), we take the shoe and symbolically *offer* it to our pup: With the shoe in front of its mouth, we say 'LEAVE IT' and take the shoe away - but we *don't* hide it from our puppy's view.

We repeat this procedure and command until our dog either looks away or at us, even if just briefly. Immediately at that moment we praise our pup verbally ('GOOD - LEAVE IT'), *and* give a designated Chew Toy instead - ie we must have it ready to hand before we walk to our puppy to take the shoe away.

Perfect would be if we can now in addition give a Real-Life Reward (p~132) because this would provide immediate positive distraction (although young puppies do not yet consciously associate the two).

We repeat the entire sequence above whenever our puppy chews something it's not supposed to chew. This also is a great training of the 'LEAVE IT' command, because ideally any dog commands should be trained in the relevant situation.

Whichever approach of the two you choose, important is that you do nothing else, particularly don't be resentful. Because a puppy cannot relate your mood to its own prior behavior.

3) If you feel you cannot invest the consistency and persistence that is necessary for the above puppy **training** approaches, then you can (in addition) resort to anti-chew remedies.

The **top anti-chew remedies** that can help to prevent that your puppy chews items it's not supposed to chew are (arguably, with *increasing* effectiveness):

- Bitter Apple Spray: mygermanshepherd.org/go/bitter-apple-spray

- Nilodor Anti Chew Spray: mygermanshepherd.org/go/nilodor-anti-chew-spray

- Virbac Stop Crib paste: bit.ly/1bhPLJJ (meant for horses, but works well for dogs too; possible alternative spray: mygermanshepherd.org/go/crib-stop-spray)

- Tabasco: mygermanshepherd.org/go/tabasco (yes!)

- Cayenne Pepper: mygermanshepherd.org/go/cayenne-pepper (dust it, or mix with water or olive oil to spray or glaze, or with vaseline to get a paste)

- Sentry Stop That: mygermanshepherd.org/go/sentry-stop-that (a pheromone combination, but after the first couple of times just showing the bottle is probably enough)

Note though that the effectiveness of the above remedies *varies* with the individual dog. For example, some puppies seem almost to *like* Bitter Apple Spray. In such case just try another remedy to prevent your pup from chewing items it isn't supposed to chew.

And some remedies we certainly don't want to have on some of our items (say Tabasco on table legs or clothes). But the above list leaves enough options - with Sentry Stop That apparently being the most powerful remedy to correct undesirable puppy behavior.

Puppy Scratching

Similarly to chewing, never try to stop puppy scratching entirely because a puppy must also use its paws and claws for them to develop well.

Again, to prevent your puppy scratching on your table legs, antique furniture etc, first give your puppy some alternatives.

Suitable dog scratch mats are rarely sold as such, but you can simply use one of those hardwearing quality door entry mats (mygermanshepherd.org/go/scratch -doormat) that are made of non-toxic polypropylene fiber and are easy to clean.

Apply the same reward mechanism as in the prior chapter, and use *positive* reinforcement dog training only (ie never punish for scratching - you would practically punish your dog's genetical heritage).

In addition, unless you have some serious problem with that, *do* allow your pup to dig in the garden. Digging is not just a great energy release, it also strengthens paws and claws. Some dog breeds have a genetic quest for digging, and I see no problem with that.

Step 2 and 3 (Training and Remedies) are the same as for Puppy Chewing (p~212).

Puppy Digging

Unless you have some serious problem with that, *do* allow your pup to dig in the garden. **Digging** is not just a great energy release, it also strengthens paws and shortens claws *naturally*. Some dog breeds have a genetic quest for digging, and I see no problem with that.

I haven't yet succeeded in teaching our dogs to dig up something of value (I was hoping for gold, jewellery, coins, notes, and the like), but maybe you can. In such case, by all means, please do let me know! :-)

Conversely, IF you have a problem with excessive digging, you can proceed as follows:

1. Identify and then mark an area where digging shall be allowed. - No need to build something fancy, you can put up a simple 'barrier' around that, like say a ribbon spanning across poles, leaving one side open (ideally use a bright yellow or bright blue color since this is the canine color spectrum)

2. Train your pup to respect the barrier (see in a second)

3. Thereafter, when your pup is digging in a forbidden area, walk up to your dog, point your finger down on that forbidden area while saying a short sharp "NO Digging here", and then do the Collar Freeze (p~142).

Important: If our puppy repetitively digs in that *same* spot again, we can consider it as *consistent misconduct* and we can use Isolation (p~145) in future. But if our puppy digs in *another* forbidden area, then - from a dog's viewpoint - this is a *different* environment, and thus from our viewpoint a *new* misconduct.

Therefore, we better start afresh with the Collar Freeze (p~142) for a few times (if necessary). It's just fair, as from our dog's viewpoint (s)he couldn't know that the chosen *new* spot is forbidden too.

Remember: Dogs' ability to abstract is small. They do not easily relate behavior in *one* situation or environment to that in *another* situation or environment. And we cannot know how narrow our puppy defines 'the same environment', as this depends on age and puppy development, as well as many other factors.

How We Train Our Dog to Respect a Barrier

This chapter gives another sneak preview on our **Behavior Training**, which in its extreme form is for adult dogs (and maybe mature puppies). Because young puppies do not yet observe our own behavior as diligently as adult dogs certainly do.

Thus, whether or not the following steps help your puppy training depends on age and puppy development stage (as well as *how* you do it, of course).

Since we have just put up a cheap *indicative* barrier to manage Puppy Digging (instead of building a physical barrier), of course we now need to train our pup to *respect* such a barrier.

Here's one way how to do that, and if it works for you, then probably without the need for any command at all:

- Lead your pup into the garden, and demonstratively look down on your creative barrier while pointing your finger at it

- While demonstratively looking down at it, take a giant step over the barrier into a *forbidden area* to indicate the difficulty or impossibility for a small puppy to cross it

- Now in that *forbidden area*, demonstratively look down and point your finger down on the ground, then look up at your pup and say a short sharp "NO Digging here" while still pointing your finger down at the forbidden area (instead of waving your finger at your pup in a parent-child manner)

- Next, again while demonstratively looking down at it, take a giant step over the barrier into the *allowed area* to indicate the difficulty or impossibility for a small puppy to cross it

- Now in the *allowed area*, demonstratively look down and point your finger down on the ground, then look up at your pup and say a mild and friendly "HERE Digging" (try to start with the word you stress) while still pointing your finger down at the allowed area

- From now on, always respect the 'barrier' yourself. So, go back to your pup through the side you left open ('entrance') and lead your pup into the allowed area - all while demonstratively looking down (somewhat 'scared') at the barrier around it

- Now, with your puppy next to you, again demonstratively look down and point your finger down on the ground, then look up at your pup and say a mild and friendly "HERE Digging"

- Make a FUN theater performance out of all this, yes!

You may need to give this *performance* a few times over the span of a few days, but if you do this well, your dog will now certainly *halt* before the barrier, wondering: "Gosh, what is that yellow thing here that makes crossing this area so much more difficult now??".

This alone will not necessarily *stop* your puppy from crossing the indicative barrier and digging in the forbidden area, but it will certainly make your dog *halt* and *think*. - That's our first goal achieved!

If I then see that our puppy attempts to cross the barrier, *then* I would use a second cue.

For example, I would demonstratively enter the allowed area through the open side (as always, while demonstratively looking down at the barrier). Then I'd turn round, look down at the barrier (somewhat 'scared'), and point my finger down. Then I'd look up at our pup and stretch out my arm with the flat palm of my hand signaling the 'barrier' to our dog more vividly.

If that's still not enough, *then* I might proceed with step 3 in the prior chapter Puppy Digging (p~217), ie ending up with the Collar Freeze (p~142).

The last resort again would be Isolation (p~145) - and without doubt, a couple of Isolations will then certainly end the digging. It will work even quicker when our puppy realizes that digging in one part of the marked garden has no consequences, while digging in all other parts of the garden leads to a separation of its Pack - something no dogs like! This is another reason why you should allow digging in a marked area.

In short: Rather than *reactive* behavior modification (through Collar Freeze and Isolation), our adult dog **Behavior Training** has its focus on *proactively* shaping the behavior of our dog (through leading by example).

Show - Don't Tell

Because dog language is ... ... body language, yes!

In any case, if you consistently *behave* like this for a while (demonstratively respecting the 'barrier' yourself, signaling "NO Digging here" in the forbidden area, and signaling "HERE Digging" in the allowed area), then your puppy's mind will facilitate a new neuronal connection that tells the dog that the garden has 'changed'.

Although it hasn't really. We didn't have to *build* a barrier, and we didn't have to prevent our puppy from entering the garden either.

More importantly:

- We didn't have to use force
- We didn't have to raise fear
- We didn't have to shout
- We didn't have to push or pull our dog out
- We didn't have to set up an electronic shock or sound exclusion zone
- Most likely, we didn't even have to *command* our dog.

By avoiding all of the above, we also ensured that we remain a *pleasant* experience for our pup - which is necessary for the Recall (p~127) to work reliably.

Puppy Barking

First, note that a healthy puppy <u>must</u> bark every now and then. It's part of being a dog, a canine. We should never aim to stop puppy barking altogether, instead we should merely control when our puppy barks, and for how long.

Second, please note that no dog and no puppy 'barks for no reason' - like many dog owners are complaining. A dog *always* has a good reason why it barks, and the same is true for a puppy. Sometimes the barking may even be in our own best interest - we just don't yet notice or accept the reason.

Though, what is a 'good reason' for the puppy may not always be a good reason in our human thinking, particularly if we haven't learned to focus on what a dog may be noticing when it barks.

The <u>key causes of barking</u> are:

- Barking for Attention
- Anxiety Barking
- Alarm Barking

Barking for Attention

To make it short, Barking for Attention we don't want at all, because if we give in here we would communicate to our puppy that our pup is the Pack leader - who can determine when it gets attention.

So, the best is to ignore all barking if, after reading this entire chapter, we believe that our pup just wants attention, and if we are sure that our puppy doesn't need to urinate, or needs water or food.

If the barking goes on for what we feel is unbearable, then we revert to the Collar Freeze (p~142) or Isolation (p~145), in this order.

Anxiety Barking

Anxiety Barking happens when our pup feels anxious, whether it's Separation Anxiety, Car Anxiety, or any other anxiety. Anxiety causes our puppy to become *restless, nervous,* or even *aggressive.* Therefore, when our puppy feels anxious, it takes barking as a means of **releasing negative energy**.

Such pent-up energy in our dog needs a positive way out, otherwise our dog will bark and bark and bark - until it is dehydrated and has no more energy, or until the neighbors have called the police.

The most positive way to release energy is exercise! Our puppy will never bark because of anxiety if we make it exercise until it is tired from exhaustion! Yes, it is that simple.

For both, Anxiety Barking and Barking for Attention, the most effective way to *proactively* stop excessive barking is to provide our puppy with **much more exercise**.

The trouble is if we don't have time for this (or if the weather is too bad). Then there is almost no other possibility to *proactively* stop barking, because almost all dog training equipment or dog agility equipment is either:

- not suitable for small and young puppies, and/or

- it is very expensive, and/or
- we have to observe our pup while exercising

If money is not a prime concern, this puppy tread-mill (mygermanshepherd.org/go/puppy-mini-pacer-treadmill) is suitable for exercising puppies (and their sister product (mygermanshepherd.org/go/dog-pacer-treadmill) even for the largest dogs), but I doubt we can leave our pup alone with it, even if treadmill-trained. Also, a treadmill is just for indoor use.

The only exercise instrument I know of that we *can* leave a dog alone with for a while, outdoors as well as indoors (in a room with no furniture), is the Varsity Ball (mygermanshepherd.org/go/varsity-ball). Because it's indestructible, not-disintegrating, and too large to be swallowed. It's actually comparatively cheap too.

However, the Varsity Ball cannot be recommended for young or small puppies. I'd say minimum age is 6 months and minimum height from paw pad to top of shoulder blade is 20 inches (mygermanshepherd.org/how-to-measure-your-dogs-height-and-weight shows how to measure your pup correctly).

Also, initial observation is a must since agitated Play with the Varsity Ball is extremely exhausting.

The most effective way to *reactively* stop excessive Anxiety Barking and Barking for Attention is to perform the Collar Freeze (p~142) or Isolation (p~145), in this order.

SSCD (p~116) is less suitable for this purpose, unless we use it to lead our pup away from whatever is causing anxiety.

Alarm Barking

Particularly puppies from guard dog breeds will typically start to alarm us consciously from age 10 to 12 weeks onwards when they notice something that they think deserves our immediate attention.

Puppies may see or hear someone or something unusual and strange, and they will start to bark. And often, they won't easily stop.

Alarm Barking is very helpful, and thus we shouldn't want to curb it altogether. Instead, the best is to manage Alarm Barking effectively; this response is actually taken directly from Dan Abdelnoor's own approach (mygermanshepherd.org/go/online-dog-trainer) - we recommend him because of his superior dog training approach:

If our puppy barks when it sees a stranger coming or something unusual is happening which we feel might become a real danger (in future), then we praise our pup briefly: We walk to our puppy, get in front of it, look in the same direction, and then briefly say 'Thank you'. Without looking at our pup, or patting it, or saying anything in addition. We then simply go back to do whatever we were doing. - If barking continues, we do the same *one more time*, but afterwards we respond with immediate Isolation (p~145).

If our puppy barks for any reason which we feel cannot become a real danger (in future), then we *ignore* our pup: We do not walk to our puppy, we do not speak to it, and we do not touch it either. We completely ignore our pup. This may be hard at first if our puppy doesn't seem to stop barking, but the payoff in future is great: No more barking in such situations!

If we feel we need to, we just go in another room for a while or listen to music on headphones. Because, ideally we don't isolate our puppy in this second situation:

Since we feel it cannot become a real danger (in future), best is to make nothing of it. If we make nothing of it, our pup will soon realize that it need not alarm us about it.

Conversely, if we were to send our pup into Isolation (p~145) in this situation, we would give it weight. Plus, if we have a protective puppy, it would 'go mad' in isolation because now it cannot protect us! This would lead to intense Separation Anxiety.

So, really, best is to make nothing of it, if we feel it cannot become a real danger (in future).

Puppy Whining

Puppy whining can quickly get very annoying, and you may want to make it part of your Puppy Behavior Training (p~210) to curb *excessive* whining straight away.

In that case please be aware though: Puppy whining too is a natural part of puppy development. So, regardless *why* your pup is whining (see reasons below), you *shouldn't* try to eliminate it completely.

Whining is the non-verbal form of dog communication:

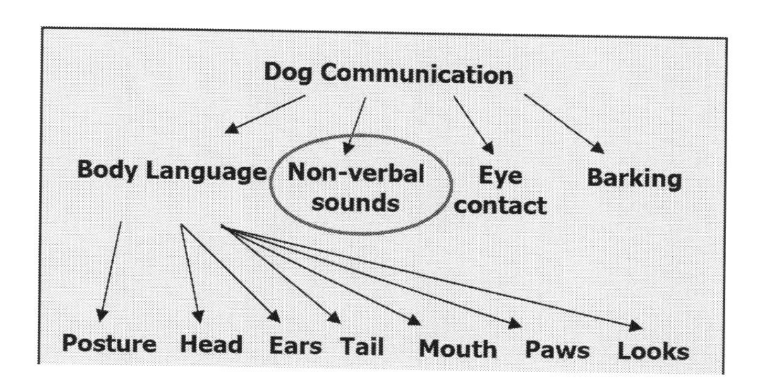

Like we humans won't always speak clearly in order to express our feelings, canines won't always bark in order to communicate their feelings. And, most dog owners (and neighbors) are glad about this fact. ;-)

Try to notice *why* your puppy is whining, and address the cause, not the symptom.

Typically, a whining puppy has one of the following reasons:

- Puppy is ill
- Puppy suffers pain and tries to inform us or to use the whining to serve as a valve
- Puppy is hungry or thirsty
- Puppy needs to go potty immediately
- Puppy feels anxious
- Puppy seeks attention

Assuming you regularly look after your puppy's food, water, and potty needs anyway (and that your pup is not ill or in pain), the likely cause of puppy whining is Attention Seeking.

In such case, if the whining is becoming excessive, aim to *ignore* it (see Puppy Attention Seeking, p~98). Go in another room, or use some excellent headphones with noise cancelling (mygermanshepherd.org/go/noise-cancelling-headphones).

However, first consider whether your pup might be whining due to feeling anxious. Particularly in the first few weeks when you get a new puppy, *everything* is new - *and* your pup lost its litter mates (dog pack)!

While many people argue that canines don't feel sad about loss like we do (or even that dogs have no long-term memory!), I disagree. Based on many close observations I am *certain* that dogs do feel sad about loss too.

More: I am certain that dogs *feel* the difference between dog pack and human family pack.

Not in the sense that our puppy would know from looking in the mirror that it just lost its pack that looked very similar to itself, and got a pack that looks very different (us).

Why *not* in that sense? Because dogs don't care much about looks (here you can see what dogs see: mygermanshepherd.org/periodical/gsd-eye-care). Also, you know that dogs feel no more attracted to a dog owner like Richard Gere or Paris Hilton than to a homeless man on the street - subject to being treated equally).

But in the sense that all of us *smell* very different to how our puppy's dog pack used to smell (and how other dogs smell that our pup meets).

Why in *that* sense? Because dogs navigate the world primarily by smell (at close range) and hearing (at a distance), ie not visually, like we do.

In this regard: If you want to know more about dog psychology, what dogs are feeling, and what they are likely thinking, I can recommend to get a broader picture with books from Stanley Coren, in particular:

- Born to Bark (mygermanshepherd.org/go/book-born-to-bark)
- The Intelligence of Dogs - A Guide to the Thoughts, Emotions, and Inner Lives of Our Canine Companions (mygermanshepherd.org/go/book-intelligence-of-dogs-emotions)
- How Dogs Think - Understanding the Canine Mind (mygermanshepherd.org/go/book-how-dogs-think)

Anyway, back to the necessary check whether our puppy might feel anxious. How can we rule out anxiety - such that we can be reasonably certain that our pup's excessive whining is 'just' Attention Seeking?

Is there a specific 'whining tone' that reveals the cause of the whining?

You may laugh at this if you are new to having dogs, but *yes*, if we bring enough *consciousness* into our dog-human relationship then over time we can indeed *hear* the difference - or at least we have the impression of hearing it, as we subconsciously also consider a whole array of other indicators of our pup's well-being, eg:

- How long have we had our puppy?
- Was it a rescue or a 'normal' upbringing?
- Did the last meal contain some irregular/new foods?
- Is our pup running around while whining?
- Somewhat scouring over the floor?
- Have we locked away our pup?
- Does the whining stop when we hold our pup?
- Does it stop when we walk our dog?
- etc.

You notice already: In the first couple of weeks or so, before we feel we know our puppy well and can *hear* differences in how it feels, it is sensible to give our pup 'the benefit of the doubt' and *act* on excessive whining, rather than ignoring it.

In addition, similar to small children, young puppies are most of the time *very* dependent and do need almost non-stop attention and love anyway in order to develop well (that's why I wrote *'just'* attention seeking with apostrophes).

Finally, *both* whining because of feeling anxious and whining because of seeking attention are ultimately a result of being **bored**:

A puppy right in the middle of exercise or exciting playtime won't whine for either of these reasons. ;-)

Puppy Jumping

Why do pups jump up?

- out of excitement
- to get up to the level of our face
- to signal their presumed dominance

Most people who find a bouncy dog annoying do so out of fear: Because a dog that's jumping up gets its mouth (and teeth) closer to our face.

No matter how much we love our puppy, the closing in of mouth and teeth - together with the fast motion of jumping - is not a feeling of comfort (to *any* living being).

An additional 'don't like it' factor is that "what jumps up has to come down", due to gravity. So, if our pup is stretching its front legs for a jump in the direction of our legs (if small puppy) or our chest (if large puppy) then its front claws will land where? Yes, right in our legs or chest!

Whether our pup was just wading through mud or not, has short claws or not, and has lots of pushing power or not - we may not exactly love such jumping.

If you find puppy jumping annoying, you can seek to limit it to certain situations like say, not jumping up on you or guests but only through a foam-covered hula hoop as agility exercise (mygermanshepherd.org/go/foam-covered-hula-hoop).

However, you shouldn't attempt to eliminate puppy jumping entirely: Jumping is part of their play, it is training and improving their agility, and it also is an indication of both physical and mental health as well as an indication of an upbeat mood in your presence! Indeed, all very positive points you could argue.

On the other hand, when you have guests a bouncy pup can be embarassing, and when you have small children a bouncy pup can even become a danger.

So, how can we train our puppy *not* to jump up?

1. Do not greet your puppy with the same level of excitement it shows itself, instead counter-balance its behavior. This means, if your pup jumps up out of excitement to have your attention, reduce the amount of attention you give.

2. Meet your pup at its own level of height. This means, if your puppy jumps up to greet you closer to your face (where your eyes are and from where you speak), bend down to greet your pup on a level slightly above its own head.

3. Going forward, use all jump situations to train your pup basic dog commands like 'NO', 'SIT', 'DOWN', and 'OFF' - and to train yourself to react to jumping the *right* way, as follows.

4. Whenever our pup jumps up (on us or on other people), we should turn so much *sideways* that our body language is uninviting - but that we can still see what our pup (or anyone's dog!) is doing.

5. So, we *don't* turn the back on our puppy (or anyone's dog) - this is rude (and in case of another person's dog it would signal that we have no respect, which is a dangerous signal to give to a dog).

6. Instead, we turn *sideways*, fold the arms, and ignore the jumping (ie not even looking at our pup).

7. If our puppy (or anyone's dog) is too strong and the jumping threatens us to fall over, we *briefly* seek eye contact, say a sharp 'NO!', and demonstratively *walk away*.

8. If we can, before our pup (or anyone's dog!) comes close, we calmly but firmly say 'SIT!' (and then 'DOWN' if we want, because from a 'down' position dogs *cannot* jump up, while from a 'sit' position they can).

9. If we reacted too late and the front paws are already resting on our legs or chest, we calmly but firmly say 'OFF!'.

10. Of course, to all above voice commands we should add an appropriate visual cue when we say the command (eg a sweeping index finger pointing at 2 o'clock and downwards to support the 'OFF' command, or whatever you choose; you can record it nicely in the Commands Little Helper, p~170).

11. Whenever our puppy greets *without* jumping, we reward with *calm* praise and/or affection.

12. We never reward with increased attention for jumping up. Increased attention includes inconspicuous matters like merely looking at our pup and saying "Stop jumping". - This as well is giving attention!

We continue this training until our puppy is totally compliant in all situations and environments. Because you saw already under Leash Training (Stage 3, p~122) that dogs do not easily relate trained behavior in one situation and environment to the required behavior in another situation and environment.

Puppy Mouthing and Nipping

Many dog owners, trainers, and authors consider **puppy mouthing and nipping** as *playful*, but **biting** as *willful* harm.

While I can agree with the first, I disagree with the second (about biting). While we must prevent all forms of *biting*, mouthing and nipping actually do provide significant benefits to puppy development. Thus although a mere mouthing and nipping can be unpleasant for us (already a *puppy's* mouth can be intimidating), we should not curb it outright.

Indeed, as long as we control the **mouthing and nipping**, this *natural* canine puppy behavior is so beneficial that we should encourage it!

Before you fall off your chair in disbelief, read on to see why.

First, the differences between mouthing and nipping.

Mouthing

Mouthing is best understood as what a lion in a circus is doing with the presenter's head. Remember that child memory?

The lion is opening its mouth wide, and - with big ballyhoo from the drums - the presenter dares to position his own head right inside the lion's mouth! If it's a *good* circus show, the lion will even slowly close its mouth enough to have the teeth touch the presenter's head. Gosh!

As children we were in awe, but in reality this performance isn't dangerous at all: The lion got what you give your puppy from now on - Bite Inhibition Training (p~162).

So, **mouthing** means our puppy clasps something or some body part with its jaws without applying any bite force at all. Like at that moment when dogs are *carrying* an item in their mouth, for example a *Soft* Floppy disc (mygermanshepherd.org/go/dog-activity-toys-floppy-disc) after FETCH.

Nipping

Nipping is a good degree more: Our puppy clasps something or some body part with its jaws and applies enough bite force to make a living object (animal or human) feel a pinch.

Don't worry about this, it is not meant to be mean at all. This is *natural* canine puppy behavior, similar to when babies start to grab with their hands. But unlike that, even a toy breed pup's pointed baby teeth can hurt!

That's why during Play with our puppy we *shouldn't* wear thick clothes, because then we can't assess the bite force our pup applies.

You may be thinking: "But thick clothes would protect me", right?

This book is about Puppy training, and this training should start *immediately* when we get our pup (see When to Start Puppy Training, p~79). Then there is no chance for our pup to develop a bite force that could hurt us more than a small pinch.

Why Controlled Mouthing and Nipping is Great

All three (mouthing, nipping, and biting) mark distinctly different stages of Bite Inhibition Training (p~162):

- A puppy will first start **nipping**
- Our reaction should transform this to mere **mouthing**
- This training ultimately prevents **biting**.

That's why, in general, mouthing and nipping is great! But we don't want to be mouthed and nipped all the time, right? So, how do we control our pup's use of its mouth?

By only allowing it during dedicated Puppy Play sessions (p~165), ie when we **invited** our pup to play (we called it to us). Remember: Play is a Reward (p~132).

How to Stop Uninvited Mouthing and Nipping

If you experience *uninvited* nipping or mouthing (outside dedicated Play sessions, p~165), then I suggest to proceed as follows - in line with The NO-Force, NO-Fear, NO-Fuss Puppy Training:

1. Upon the first uninvited nipping or mouthing attempt, ideally we turn away or walk away. Where not possible, we *gently* move our pup away, using the *outside* of our arm (or otherwise hand) in a *calm* movement (note that an attempt is enough)

2. Upon the second uninvited nipping or mouthing attempt, we apply the Collar Freeze (p~142). Usually this will stop the mouthing and nipping (for that moment).

3. If not, upon the third uninvited nipping or mouthing attempt, we immediately but without any rush lead our pup into Isolation (p~145).

Note: While we do either of the above, we do not speak, we do not touch, and we do not look at our puppy. We just gently do as described above (up to and including the temporary ignoring after Isolation where needed).

With some puppies this results in an immediate behavior modification for the same day (not forever just yet), but most puppies need a series of Isolations before they too finally stop their nipping and mouthing outside dedicated Play sessions (remember why not to prevent it in general, p~241).

Every puppy does get the message at some point. You may well be surprised how quickly your pup gets the message - if you proceed as described above.

This really is enough. It's all we need to do in order to stop uninvited puppy mouthing and nipping effectively.

How to Avoid to Stop Mouthing and Nipping Altogether

Make sure that you don't curb mouthing and nipping altogether (p~241)!

So, never use either of our two means of behavior modification (p~138) after you have called your puppy to you. Only ever use them when you walked to your puppy. This is crucial.

Remember: When you call your puppy to you, you *must* have a great experience for your dog (a Reward), and the type of Reward (p~132) must be a surprise.

So, the above also means: Whenever you call your puppy to you, be mentally prepared for potential mouthing and nipping - because your pup can't know *why* you called.

Clear? Good! :-)

Even when you call your puppy to get a *different* Reward, but your pup then mouths or nips you, then *don't* be upset about being nipped! Remember, it's a *natural* part of Puppy Play, and puppies expect to play all the time.

Instead, "bear it" - even if the nipping hurts. If it hurts too much, it means your pup is too excited. Then you can use the Sedatives in the Dog Training

Toolkit (mygermanshepherd.org/go/dog-training-toolkit) to calm down your pup.

Whatever you do to avoid or limit the pain from nipping, don't give your pup the impression that nipping and mouthing is now forbidden too (when you called your dog to you).

Indeed, again this highlights that it helps our puppy training A LOT when our behavior gives our dog clear and consistent signals what we want.

Example:

- We call our pup to us
- Our pup cannot know *why* (because we have a surprise)
- Our pup came, and *now* our behavior reveals what we want
- In this case, say we kneel or sit down and then make a quick double pat on our thighs. This would mean: "Come sweetie, play with me"
- And once we turn away or get up and walk away, this would mean: "Enough"

As you notice, this is exactly in line with How to Stop Uninvited Mouthing and Nipping (p~245).

Puppy Biting

Biting is another good degree more. A bite is marked by a laceration of the skin. In addition to the infection risk(!), even a toy breed pup's bite will really hurt!

Biting is serious misconduct, regardless of age. Nonetheless, I believe that most of the time biting is either a sign of *fear* or a demonstration of *dominance* - yes, even within the family pack. With a young puppy it is rather out of fear (certainly until the end of Family Socialization, p~66).

Unlike many dog trainers and authors, I believe that even **biting** a family pack member is *not* willful harm (dogs have the inherent desire to be *with* their Pack, not to harm it).

Either way, a biting puppy has not *accepted* us as Pack leader. Proof: In the dog pack the *accepted* Pack leader never gets bitten by a pack member, not even dominated by a pack member.

So, we certainly better curb biting attempts straight away. Thankfully, our puppy training approach makes this very easy indeed.

How to Stop a Puppy from Biting

Stopping puppy biting does not require anything other than the same approach that we just saw in How to Stop Uninvited Mouthing and Nipping (p~245).

The only difference is that we have to be more strict, because we do not want **biting** for *any* reason (whether fear, dominance, or anything else). We certainly don't want a fearful pup, and not a dominant pup either.

On top of this, if we consider that puppy **biting** is the most painful, and that a grown-up dog will ultimately bite even stronger, it's clear that we must not for a single time tolerate a biting puppy. So, we leave the first two steps out, as shown in the following chapter.

How to Stop Puppy Biting Immediately

Upon the first biting attempt, we immediately but *without any rush* lead our pup into Isolation (p~145).

While doing so, we do not speak, we do not touch, and we do not look at our pup. We just calmly lead our puppy into Isolation, exactly as described in that chapter.

Now what is important to understand is that although there should be zero tolerance for a biting puppy, we do *not* show any form of aggression ourselves - like so many dog owners do in such situations:

They hit the pup or shout and scold, or they push or pull the puppy away, and along with this their entire body language too communicates aggression or anger. This is bad, very bad.

Instead, what we should do is, we stay *calm* (as much as we can, if the bite hurts severely) and without any rush we lead our puppy into Isolation. Nothing else.

Why is Isolation so Effective?

Isolation is so effective because it directly addresses the second-most fundamental canine quest (p~92): The inherent canine desire to belong to a Pack - to either be an accepted Pack member or the accepted Pack leader!

An isolated puppy or adult dog instinctively realizes that it is excluded from a Pack, any Pack. No canine likes this, because it goes against their genetical heritage. In fact, I don't know of any breed where the breeders have successfully eliminated this canine quest (see also the note under Puberty, p~68).

This is exactly the reason why shelter dogs of shelters where the staff have not enough time to socialize with every abandoned dog and where the dogs are kept individually, within a mere days 'go nuts' (quite literally):

The exclusion from any Pack, exacerbated by the whining and yowling of the neighboring dogs (which by the way communicates their suffering from being excluded from any Pack), puts terrible strain on these shelter dogs.

If you doubt this, you may want to visit a few shelters, some where shelter staff can socialize with the dogs at least a bit every now and then, and some where they cannot, and where the dogs are kept individually. Or, maybe, if you read this (examiner.com/article/don-t-breed-or-buy-while-shelter-pets-die) it's enough to convince you. It's the uncut version of the widespread 'Letter of a Shelter Manager' which hasn't yet been seen by all prospective puppy buyers and actual dog owners.

But maybe you wonder: If Isolation (p~145) directly addresses the second-most fundamental canine quest (p~92), isn't it then a means 'too cruel' to be applied to a puppy?

This is human thinking but, as much as we know, not how dogs think. For dogs and puppies, the short isolation is just the right amount of feedback - which they would get in their dog pack too:

When you watch Litter Socialization (p~65), you can observe exactly the same. When a pup has 'gone too far', mum and litter mates ignore it for a while. Depending on the puppy development stage, this can range from 'turning their back on it', to moving it away.

Our Isolation and subsequent ignoring is short too. Most of the time it will not even take an hour to get our puppy back on track.

How to Stop Puppy Biting Proactively

While Isolation (p~145) is an easy and effective response to a biting puppy, note that we merely react in a given situation after our puppy has bitten or attempted to bite (whether family pack member or third party). Indeed, Isolation does its job well to stop biting *in a given situation.*

But ideally, we better proactively train our pup not to bite in any situation. This approach would be so much better, because:

- It would *prevent* biting in the first place
- It would safeguard us from shock and pain bites
- It would give us peace of mind
- It would make our children safe (and other children and other pets too)

Therefore, we must find a better solution. That better solution is regular and systematic Bite Inhibition Training as described earlier (p~162).

Puppy Aggression

Forms of Aggression

Aggressive puppy biting we address as described under How to Stop Puppy Biting Immediately (p~251).

For other forms of aggression in puppies we try to identify the cause of the aggressive puppy behavior.

We may be dealing with:

- Dog on Dog aggression
- Dominance aggression (pup thinks it is Pack leader)
- Fear aggression
- Food aggression
- Lead aggression
- Sudden aggression (due to pain or illness)
- Territorial aggression (again, pup thinks it is Pack leader)

We don't want any form of aggression - and if we believe it may be sudden aggression due to pain or illness, then of course we try to *help* our puppy: visiting the vet, giving a good canine pain relief (mygermanshepherd.org/go/canine-pain-relief), or simply a lot of rest.

Eliminating Aggression

Again, we proceed as described earlier for the puppy problems: We respond with the Collar Freeze (p~142) or Isolation (p~145).

You may not believe this if you just *read* it without actually *applying* it, but these two means really are totally sufficient!

The Collar Freeze is particularly effective to heal Dog on Dog aggression, Fear aggression, Food aggression, and Lead aggression. Lead aggression can also be eliminated using SSCD (p~116) alone.

Dominance aggression and Territorial aggression is most effectively dealt with using Isolation.

Now you may wonder: How do I know which aggression it is?

Dog on Dog aggression, Food aggression, and Lead aggression are obvious anyway (other dog, food, or lead involved). To identify Territorial aggression, Dominance aggression, or Fear aggression we need to closely observe the situation and read the body language of our dog.

But this would now really go way beyond this **Puppy Development Guide - Puppy 101**. I am working on my own book on dog body language, but until then, a good *pictured* book on **dog body**

language is Canine Body Language (mygermanshep herd.org/go/canine-body-language).

And in order to tackle aggression issues of your pup, you *don't* need to become an expert in reading dog body language. Best is to simply respond with the Collar Freeze (p~142) or Isolation (p~145), in this order - and you will successfully eliminate all forms of puppy aggression!

I truly doubt it but should you face a problem with your puppy despite **applying** all the advice found in this **Puppy Development Guide - Puppy 101**, then please do send me an email to support@mygermanshepherd.org, because I am happy to help. But do mention that you read this book - or your message is likely to end up in the daily spam flood we are getting on our site as well! :-(

Puppy Training -v- Relationship Building

Relationship building with our puppy is far more important than pure puppy training - whether obedience training or training our puppy some tricks (for this, by the way, a great book is training 101 dog tricks: mygermanshepherd.org/go/101-dog-tricks).

Don't worry, with 'Relationship Building' I don't mean to develop our puppy to become an equal partner for us/ in our family. That would go too far for most of us dog lovers, wouldn't it?

But likewise, I don't mean to raise an 'obedient' puppy either. We don't want a dog that's our slave, 'executing' our commands all the time. Or do you?

No, with Relationship Building I mean to raise a dog that we appreciate for what it is: A canine *animal*, but one with unprecedented abilities and motivation to *please* us.

Yes, really, that's what has been bred into dogs over up to 33,000 years: A vast variety of abilities and a huge motivation to *please* us.

The minimum we can, and should, give back is that we appreciate our dog as exactly this: A canine *animal*, but one with unprecedented abilities and motivation to *please* us.

I am a grateful person, and I am incredibly grateful for every day our dogs are with us. And so will you, when you unleash your puppy's **immense potential**!

Unleash, I like that (hence why I called the Complete Leash Training Guide Dogs Unleashed - From On-Leash to Off-Leash).

If now the only thing that hinders you is to have a *real* dog trainer by your side (a professional, not a TV entertainer...), then I can only refer to Dan Abdel-noor's online video library (mygermanshepherd.org/go/online-dog-trainer) of real daily dog and puppy training situations - and solutions.

So much better than the ordinary youtube stuff! And so much better than the wanna-be 'gurus' of dog trainers in the market... - who charge you *hundreds* of dollars for just *one* training session!

Dan uses a similar approach to ours (gentle, no force, no fear), and - with a smart phone, i-pad, kindle, nook, or kobo in your hand - you can even watch and hear *what* he does, and *how*, while you are outside dog walking! We did that too :-)

In any case, give your puppy the kind of puppy training (s)he deserves. Build a great relationship with your pup, based on this mindset. It will last a dog's lifetime!

And you will then be so thrilled to have your dog, that you will never want to give the dog to a shelter.

- But you may want to get your puppy from a shelter (p~37).

What do you think?

Puppy 101 in a Nutshell

Meanwhile this book has become so big that I thought you may appreciate to have a final summary of the key points that I feel we *must* observe to build the best relationship with our dog?

So here it is:

- Be calm before you engage with your puppy
- If you can't, perform the Collar Freeze (this will calm down both of you)
- Respect your puppy for being an animal, not a human child (but one with unbelievable abilities to bring you joy!)
- Avoid boredom by all means (exercise is great!)
- If your puppy has more energy than you (likely), use a toy like the Tail Teaser (mygermanshepherd.org/go/tail-teaser) to safely exhaust your dog while you can relax
- Whenever you call your puppy to you, have a great experience for your pup
- Be aware which reward types you can use in which situation

- Whenever you want to do sth your dog may not like, walk to your dog

- The only behavior modification needed are Isolation and the Collar Freeze (or alternatively SSCD)

- Avoid acting like a commander, aim to be the leader of the Pack (the dog pack leader doesn't bark much at all!)

- Perform the Feeding Routine exactly as described

- Ignore excessive Attention Seeking

- Use SSCD to calm down your pup before a walk, and to get the pup to match your movements already indoors

- Enjoy *controlled* Play-fighting

- Don't 'over-train' your puppy, rather use your own behavior to build a better relationship with your dog

- Use less Obedience Training, and more Behavior Training

- A lasting (great) memory for your puppy is when you have loads of FUN together! :-)

If you need ideas, see the suggested remedies on our site: mygermanshepherd.org/my-german-shepherd/mygermanshepherd-remedies/dog-play-and-exercise

~~~

And if you have an idea how to improve this **Puppy Development Guide**, please let me know:

support@mygermanshepherd.org - Thanks!

If instead or in addition you'd like to post a public review for this book, then I will definitely appreciate your review on your favorite social or bookstore platform.

~~~

Connect with Tim Carter:
https://twitter.com/mygsdorg
http://mygermanshepherd.org/comments/feed/
https://smashwords.com/interview/TimCarter
https://smashwords.com/profile/view/TimCarter
https://www.goodreads.com/TimCarter
Questions only on the website (a page where it fits the content): http://mygermanshepherd.org

More Books by the Same Author

The COMPLETE House Training Guide (mygermanshepherd.org/go/books)

House Training is so much more than housebreaking: It is everything to get your dog to behave well in the house while having free run of the house while you are away!

- "Hugely informative, there is so much stuff in here that I didnt know, and it has already helped me with my four month old puppy. Housetraining and housebreaking are truly very different things"

- "Wonderful book/guide, very simple to use methods, the results are phenomenal"

- "Excellent Guide!! Lots of great ideas and not too technical. Tim writes with the DOG in mind with emphasis on not over-thinking, over-correcting or over-training. I have used many of his methods and suggestions successfully"

- "I was amazed how much I thought I knew but really failed in my conception of family life with a GSD. The information was spot on. The book after reading it twice is a real eye opener and a MUST for dog owners"

The Complete Leash Training Guide (mygerman-shepherd.org/go/leash-training-guide)

For when your dog pulls, lunges, won't heel, runs off, or doesn't come back when you call. Even explains the equipment you need - and which you don't need!

- "Never crossed my mind to read about leash training but chuffed I did!"
- "Invaluable! This is exactly what we needed - thank you so much"

The World's Only DOG TRAINING TOOLKIT (mygermanshepherd.org/go/books)

Don't use Force, Don't use Fear, Don't Yell and Don't Shriek. Forget 'training collars' and 'treat training'. Forget Obedience Training. - **Why use *Commands* when we can use *Tools*?**

The Dog Training Toolkit revolutionizes dog training all across the globe: The *gentle* dog training approach that works even with the most difficult rescue dogs.

- "Excellent. I have tried many of the tools that Tim provides with so much success. I've had several dogs in my lifetime but have the best relationship with my GSD than with any other dog ever"

- "Great insight!"

- "This book is the most comprehensive one I have seen on training your pup/dog"

- "I've had dogs for quite a long time, both rescue and from a puppy. They've all presented unique challenges in their training and I've had to cope with it by myself. With this book you are no longer alone. It covers everything you can think of and more. I wish that this book had been available years ago when I bought my first dog from the shelter, or when I first got a puppy"

amzn.to/VrH7EN

amzn.to/WIsE6E

amzn.to/ZbARk7

amzn.to/12DCw86

Not to Forget!

1. Please do spay/neuter your puppy!

- Optimal time for neutering your male puppy: Anytime between age 6 weeks and 3 months.
- Optimal time for spaying your female puppy: Only the 4 weeks between 3 months and 4 months of age, so in month 3.
- See here why: mygermanshepherd.org/periodical/gsd-spaying-and-neutering

2. Please do visit the vet regularly. Once a year is the absolute minimum, because one year for us is between 6 and 12 years(!) for our dog (mygermanshepherd.org/german-shepherd-age-how-old-does-my-dog-think-it-is), depending on breed. The best and cheapest outcome for us is then that each time the vet concludes: "Your dog is fine!"

3. However, please do not simply nod through every treatment a vet suggests. Our aim should always be to get the correct diagnosis, and then to use the most *appropriate* treatment with the *least* long-term side effects.

- A great example: The top ear infection remedy *Zymox Otic* is available *with* hydrocortisone and *without* hydrocortisone.

- Hydrocortisone is a corticosteroid, a hormone, and as such it can have dramatic side effects with impact on seemingly unrelated body functions.

- Hence our priority should be to use Zymox Otic *without* hydrocortisone (mygermanshepherd.org/go/ear-treatment-without-cortisone)!

4. Since we are at it, before you use any ear solution, you *must* get your dog's eardrums checked by a vet: If a solution is instilled into an ear canal with a perforated eardrum, it will enter the middle ear and damage structures essential to hearing (mygermanshepherd.org/periodical/gsd-ear-care)! Then the *solution* is no 'solution' but a problem.

5. Always aim for antibiotic-free remedies.

- Do NOT get caught up in the myth that antibiotics are 'a generally suitable blanket treatment for infections'.

- No, antibiotics are a typically *unnecessary* and generally *unsuitable* treatment - and *always* lead to chronic side effects that will sooner or later become apparent!

- For almost every condition there exist more effective *natural* remedies that have *less* side effects.

- The only exception to use antibiotics: a *life-threatening* condition of our dog.

6. Consider micro-chipping your puppy: mygermanshepherd.org/periodical/micro-chipping-your-dog. Particularly puppies of certain breeds are prone to get stolen with the purpose to sell them, or dog-napped for various reasons. In any case (ie regardless where you live), puppies do commonly get lost often indeed!

7. Please do consider to get a dog from a rescue center/ shelter (p~37) - 'Do not breed or buy while shelter dogs die!'

Did I forget other important points?
Is there anything how to improve this book?
Feedback much appreciated:
mailto: support@mygermanshepherd.org -
Will add to next edition!

Most importantly, a final note:

A Puppy Quickly Becomes a Dog

and a Dog's Life is Fairly Short

so Make Sure You

ENJOY Your Dog! :-)

Every day is a chance to put things right.